MAKE YOUR SCHOOLS WORK

Practical, Imaginative and Cost-Free Plans
to Turn Public Education Around

BY Harvey B. Scribner
AND Leonard B. Stevens

Simon and Schuster / *New York*

Designed by Irving Perkins
Manufactured in the United States of America
By The Book Press, Brattleboro, Vt.

1   2   3   4   5   6   7   8   9   10

Library of Congress Cataloging in Publication Data

Scribner, Harvey B
    Make Your Schools Work.
    Bibliography: p. 127
    Includes index.
    1. Education—United States—1965— 2. Educational innovations.—United
States. I. Stevens, Leonard B., joint author. II. Title.
LA210.S386   370′.973   75-4847
ISBN 0-671-21992-8

Thanks are due the following for permission to reprint from their respective
works:
    Educational Facilities Laboratories, Inc., for permission to quote from
Schools: More Space/Less Money, a report from Educational Facilities Laboratories, 1971.
    August Gold, for permission to quote from a letter concerning the rela-
tionships between physical school environments and learning.
    The Springfield Union, Springfield, Massachusetts, for excerpts from the
article "Schools Wary of Fun Homes," January 9, 1974, reprinted from *The
Springfield Union* with permission.
    The Vermont State Department of Education, for permission to quote
excerpts from the *Vermont Design for Education,* Montpelier, Vermont,
1968, fifth reprint 1971.

For Alta and Bette

ACKNOWLEDGMENTS

The ideas and thoughts set forth in this book, while our own, are the product of many events, many years in and around schools, and of course our own collaboration. Independently and together we have borrowed and benefited over the years from more people than we could count or list; we have combined our personal debts of a general nature to each of them.

We offer special thanks to friends and supporters concerned with education in New York City, children and young people especially, who taught us more than they perhaps realize; to Diane Divoky, who initially caused us to work together; to Betty Anne Clarke, for her encouragement; to Alice Mayhew, for her faith in us; to Dan Green, for advice and help; to the University of Massachusetts and Dwight Allen; most of all to our wives, to whom this work is dedicated, for tolerating us and keeping us going.

H.B.S. / L.B.S.

Contents

Part One   THE SCHOOL PROFESSIONALS   9

Part Two   TEN PLANS FOR REFORM   19
    PLAN I   *The Birthday-Entrance Plan,* 23
    PLAN II   *The Year-Round-Learning-Center Plan,* 30
    PLAN III *The Most-Wanted-Teacher Plan,* 37
    PLAN IV   *The Apprenticed-Learner Plan,* 46
    PLAN V   *The Universal-Tutor Plan,* 51
    PLAN VI   *The Zero-Construction Building Plan,* 55
    PLAN VII *The High-School-Renewal Plan,* 66
    PLAN VIII *The Autonomous-School Plan,* 76
    PLAN IX   *The External-Diploma Plan,* 86
    PLAN X   *Bankrolled Educational Opportunity,* 93
              Make Your Own Plan, 100

Part Three THE SCHOOL LEADERS   101

Part Four   THE HOPE   115

            READING LIST   127

            INDEX   133

Part One

THE SCHOOL
PROFESSIONALS

ASK, "FOR WHOM DO THE PUBLIC SCHOOLS EXIST?" and the response invariably is, "For the young." The idea that "schools are for children" is so widespread that schools commonly are thought of as having but one purpose, the education of children; and one beneficiary, the young. Thus, for example, when schools are threatened with diminished support by state house or city hall, typically there is an outpouring of public sentiment to "save our schools." Why? To preserve public education. For whose sake? For the sake of the young. The object of saving schools is so obvious to the participants in such campaigns that it does not require spelling out.

Schools, however, serve more than one end. For society, they socialize and distribute an official culture. For the economy, they train, assort and accredit. For a democratic nation, they mold citizens. Education is only part of their business.

Nor do schools have benefits only for the young. Schools also serve those who are employed in schools, most of whom are professionals in education. These school professionals need schools at least as much as the young; perhaps more. Their jobs, their means of support, their recognition as experts and specialists, their identity as professionals depend on the existence of schools. Doctors, attorneys, architects, and the members of a score of other professions can work as individual practitioners. But not the teacher, principal or guidance counselor. For them there is no tradition of entering private practice. They need schools as places in which to practice the profession of education. Small wonder that school professionals are such consistent advocates of public schools, and such early volunteers in the "save our schools" campaigns.

Schools have traditionally depended on professionals. Now schools are dominated by them. A large class of school professionals has emerged with the expansion of public-school systems, and this class of professional now rules the schools. Public control of schools is close to a fantasy.

11

The professional class* is not an organization or a "union." Indeed this class—this body of like-minded experts—transcends the professionals' unions. It includes the top administrators of school systems, the executives and managers in the educational agencies of the state and national governments, the principals and other supervisors who constitute the middle management of the public schools, the army of classroom teachers, the counselors and other specialists, and the growing ranks of near-professionals: teacher aides, teacher assistants, paraprofessionals, school safety officers, et cetera. This class would exist and would exert its influence even without the existence of unions and other formal organizations.

Produced by the universities, certified and licensed by the state, the school professionals do more than staff the schools of America—they rule them. In turn, the schools respond to the needs and interests of this ruling class, sometimes at the expense of the needs and interests of the young. Contrary to popular belief, the public does not control the schools—the professionals do. Contrary to the belief that schools exist to serve the young, schools often work better today for the professionals employed by the schools than for the children who populate the classrooms.

The professionals believe in the ability of professionals to solve the problems that afflict schools. With money, more professionals could be hired. With more professionals, the young would get more attention. With more attention—smaller class

---

* As working professionals in education, we too are part of this class. Our attitudes, however, are not class attitudes, as should be clear. This is the issue: the existence of class attitudes and the pursuit of class interests. The target of our criticism is not each and every professional in education—there are some very good ones, obviously. What we do criticize is the dominance of schools by a class of professional at the expense of the young. In our optimistic hours we see professionals in increasing numbers taking issue with the class orientation of their own profession, and disassociating themselves from such class interests. In times of pessimism we see a very small minority of school professionals embarking on such a course of independence. At this writing we are more pessimistic than optimistic on this subject, and, therefore, we place more hope on laymen taking the initiative to reform schools. The professionals, we feel, will—as a class—fight fundamental reform proposals, because they will view them as threatening their position of dominance.

size, for example—the young would learn with greater effectiveness and efficiency. This is the perception of the school professionals. More than anything else, they believe in professionalizing schools—more professionals, more control for professionals, greater reliance on the judgment of professionals. The implications are clear: laymen (parents) do not belong in the school decision-making process; instruction must remain the exclusive privilege of professional teachers; radical changes in education are both unnecessary and undesirable; what the schools need most in the search for quality is more money.

There is a professionalized solution to virtually every problem that comes along in education. To combat reading failure, call in the reading specialists. When there is student misbehavior or evidence of poor "adjustment," bring on the guidance counselors. For emotional problems, call in the school psychologists. When the educational content of schools—"the curriculum"—is in need of repair, form a curriculum committee—of professionals. To hold down disruption, hire security guards. Are some youth not coming to school at all? Employ more attendance officers. In the perception of the professional class, problems demand more professionals, more specialists, more experts, not reform of the institution. And if the problems remain (as they inevitably do), or when they take on new symptoms, the answer is more professionals of a different kind.

The greater crime today is not that schools are so appallingly failure-ridden but that they tend so powerfully to stay the way they are. Even in the face of clear failure to meet the needs of thousands of the young, schools display an uncommon capacity to resist fundamental reform. The explanations are multiple. Bureaucracy, inertia, the constraints imposed by union contracts, lack of reform money, a general "mindlessness," public apathy—each of these explanations has a certain element of truth. But they do not explain everything.

The school professionals are indeed the ruling class in the schools, and their dominance has a good deal to do with the resistance of the schools to proposals for reform. Any dominant group seeks to retain its favored place by preserving status quo and fending off change. The school professionals are no different. The schools are working to their interests, and the professional class intends to keep the balance of power tilted in its favor. A few examples will illustrate the point:

COMMUNITY CONTROL OF SCHOOLS. The concept is based on increasing the involvement of parents in decisions concerning schools. Professionals like to speak of home-school connections, but they oppose the idea of community control. Dangerous, says Albert Shanker, who is easily the most visible and influential leader of organized school professionals in the United States.* Professionals as a class prefer to keep parents at arm's length, away from educational decisions. When school decentralization was first proposed in New York City, the professionals fought it. When it became clear that something had to be done, the professionals worked successfully to dilute the plan. Today, decentralization in New York City—what little there is of it—is in deep trouble. The professionals, as a class, can take much of the credit.

PERFORMANCE CONTRACTING. The idea of performance contracting is that when children are failing in school, it might—

* Mr. Shanker is president of the American Federation of Teachers as well as the A.F.T.'s chief local organization, the United Federation of Teachers in New York City. On occasion he will speak favorably of school *decentralization,* but never favorably of *community control* of schools. The reason is that decentralization (as in the New York City school system) is a means of dispersing some administrative authority but not much political power. Under decentralization most power remains in the hands of professionals (not laymen), and ultimate authority is retained by a central agency, typically a central school board, that usually is more attuned to the interests of professionals as a class than many community school boards would be. One impact of weak decentralization schemes—New York City's is a prime example—is that "community" school boards get little real control over schools, but they are perceived as responsible for them; failure thus becomes their responsibility, not the responsibility of the central headquarters. Decentralization thereby fails by design. The concept of community control would involve an authentic redistribution of school power in the favor of parents and other laymen. It therefore is threatening to professionals. Mr. Shanker's views, because of their consistency, represent a classic illustration of the distrust that school professionals typically hold for the idea that parents can make responsible educational decisions, and the faith professionals typically have that they (the professionals) always know best.

might—be useful to go outside the school for help, especially if help can be found from a source that says, "Don't pay us unless we teach children to learn." It may not be the most original, or even most promising, idea in school reform, but at least it is an idea that is oriented to the interests of the young. The professionals say that they are concerned with the needs of the young. But they oppose performance contracts. Educationally unsound, they say. In New York State, local public funds may not be used for performance contracts. The school professionals have seen to that.

TEACHER CERTIFICATION. Frequently it is proposed that the licenses of teachers be made subject to periodic review. The idea is to make sure that teachers continue to be fit to teach. The professionals favor competence, and surely they favor the protection of children from unfit teachers. But they oppose the proposal that teachers should be "relicensed" every few years. Unnecessary, they say. The probationary period before tenure is the time to assess fitness and to dismiss unfit teachers, they contend. We suggest that parents look at the records of their school districts on the matter of tenure. In most school districts, nearly 100 percent of the teachers who come up for tenure are granted it. The review of probationary teachers—a review conducted and controlled by professionals—is hardly a tough review. Nor does the probationary period, created to protect the young, work in the interest of the young or of the public. The same can be said of tenure.

SENIORITY RIGHTS. In most school systems seniority yields rewards. Senior teachers can virtually choose the schools in which they wish to work; at worst, they can escape from the "difficult" schools. Those who work in summer or after-school projects obtain "retention rights"—which means that they get the same job again the following year if they want it. In periods of recession, when layoffs are required, the principle of "last hired/first fired" is followed, and the more senior professionals thereby are saved. Do seniority rights have an impact on the young? Clearly they do. Do they work in the interest of the young? No; they are antithetical to the needs of the young. The children in the "worst" schools need the most competent teachers, not the least experienced. The children in summer and after-school programs ought to have the very best teachers, not those with job-preference rights. When a budget necessitates a cutback in staff, the least competent professionals ought to be dismissed, not the ones with least seniority. What is the origin of these seniority rights? The professionals demanded them, bargained for them, and they work hard to protect and extend them.

It is time for parents to be told the modern facts of life about their schools. Parents cannot shift their children from one teacher to another or choose the teachers they want for their children, because school professionals oppose. Parents cannot evaluate principals and teachers, because the professionals will not stand for it. The involvement of parents in serious school decisions is difficult to accomplish even in the most progressive school districts, because professionals, as a class, disapprove.* Proposals to allow the young to accomplish part of their education outside the schools are difficult to implement on a large scale, because the school professionals prefer to keep the young inside the schools, under their control, subject to their supervision. The idea of "external" diplomas that are equal in every way to regular high-school diplomas—so equal that they are interchangeable—is heresy to the school professionals.

The fact is that school professionals as a class represent a ma-

* While we were in New York City there was a "committee on accountability" that was working on a plan for school accountability. The committee had been established before Harvey Scribner became Chancellor. When Scribner added several persons to the committee as representatives of antipoverty and minority agencies, the representatives of the professionals' groups walked out and boycotted the committee. They stayed away for weeks, until the committee was enlarged again—with representatives of their choosing. In the interim, the pressure to remove the new antipoverty and minority representatives was intense. The pressure even came from one leading school critic who urged Scribner to compromise the issue so as to get the professionals back and to restore the committee to life. It was especially interesting to see a strong critic of failing schools arguing, in effect, for the removal of people representing precisely those families that are failed most consistently by schools.

jor obstacle to the reform of schools, because serious reform would threaten their dominance of the schools. Reform proposals that fail to recognize the existence of the professional class as a powerful force against reform are naïve and therefore doomed by their lack of perception. Reform proposals that recognize the dominance of professionals and accept it, by suggesting that professionals do indeed know best or that professionals and parents have no fundamental differences, are not proposals for reform; they are proposals that create an illusion of reform.

The ultimate test of any reform idea is: What would it do to undermine the power relations of schools, to displace the professional class from its dominant and domineering position, to empower parents to govern, to orient schools to the needs of the young? The proposals in this book are designed expressly for these purposes; and, in addition, to raise the public's consciousness of what is happening in schools. Schools ought to begin to work for the kids rather than for the professionals.

Part Two

TEN PLANS
FOR REFORM

SCHOOLS LIKE TO BE KNOWN for their openness toward change. They like to speak of their "innovation" and "experimentation." They like to inform the public of their "model" programs and "exemplary" projects. They like to show visitors their current ventures in educational "reform"—as examples of continuing progress and as evidence of their reformist attitude. In the last ten years the interest in school reform has been enormous, and (until very recently) the financial investment in the cause of reform has been unprecedented. But have the schools undergone a basic reformation? Unfortunately, they have not.

The appearance of schools is changing but not the substance. For the most part, the reform energy and money have produced new buildings, better equipped classrooms, higher salaries for teachers and administrators, a rewriting of textbooks and other educational materials, some new teaching methods, some new ways of deploying teachers and grouping children, a multitude of "demonstration" projects. But the essential character or nature of schools—"their purposes, forms and functions," as John Fischer, the former president of Teachers College, would say—has endured.

In most schools, professionals still prescribe and students still follow the prescriptions, or they fail; principals still control life inside the school walls; students still compete against each other for success; most learning is still confined inside the school and does not extend into the world beyond; parents still remain outside the decisions that affect their children and their schools. In spite of all the "reforms" of recent years, in spite of all the talk and all the money invested, these basic components or characteristics of school have remained intact. Failure too has endured. There still are dropouts. There still is massive failure in learning. And still, despite reform, there continue to be untold numbers of students who are bored by the prospect of yet another day of "education."

Is a certain amount of failure inevitable in an institution as large as the American school? We don't think so. Is failure intolerable when the young are required by law to go to school? We think it is; indeed, it would be intolerable even without compulsory education laws, in view of the emphasis this society places on education. Can anything be done? Some things have to be done.

Ten specific reform ideas follow. Each is simple. Each is practical. Each is economical. Each makes common sense (at least to us). And each plan, if adopted, has the potential to revolutionize a basic aspect of school which so many of the highly financed "reforms" of recent years have left untouched.

The obvious purpose of these ten plans is to make schools work for the young now. As should be clear, these are not the only ten plans of this kind. They are merely the first ten.

Nor is the creation of such ideas—practical plans that do not require money and have high impact—limited to school professionals. Parents—and children—are as capable as others of devising them. We hope they do. For not only is the reform of schools their right, it is also their responsibility.

PLAN I / *The Birthday-Entrance Plan*

The elements of what is called lock-step schooling are quite familiar to most people by now: the processing of children through school in groups as if they were products on a factory assembly line; the power of the textbook to standardize and homogenize learning and limit student creativity; the dictatorship of the lesson plan; competitive grades that pit one child against another and ultimately force some out of school as failures; report cards that tell the parent about where his child stands vis-à-vis other children, but little about how his child is progressing and growing as a child with unique strengths and weaknesses. This has all been described before; it is all too familiar. Familiar, too, to every parent is the school rule that says a child enters school for the first time when school reopens in September after the child's fifth or sixth birthday. (There are some exceptions to this, but this is the general rule.)

This rule, of course, is the cornerstone of the system of twelve grades that is common to virtually all schools in America. (There are thirteen grades if kindergarten is counted.) If children enter school at five or six, are grouped into grades, one through twelve, and are processed from grade to grade in groups or "classes," it is critical that they all arrive in school on the same day. Thus the rule: a child enters school for the first time the September next following his school-age birthday.

It follows that a school district can bring powerful pressure to bear against many of the elements of lock-step schooling—and strong pressure in favor of treating children as persons with individual learning programs—if it simply changes the rule concerning when children begin school. All that is required to begin to subvert the lock-step system is for a school board to declare that henceforth children shall enter school on the day of their school-age birthday—whether the day is in September or February or May, a Monday or a Friday. (As should be needless to say, the rule would say that children whose birthday falls on a weekend or a holiday would begin school on the next school day. Similarly, children whose birthday comes during the summer months when school is closed would begin school the first day of the next term.)

This plan is really more simple than the rule that most schools use now. When does a child begin school? On his or her birthday—age five if the school has a kindergarten, age six if it does not, or any other age the school board wishes to establish. What could be more simple? The teacher gains the advantage of not having to become acquainted with twenty-five or thirty new children simultaneously on the first day of school each year. Administrators can project, with as much accuracy as now, the number of children who will be arriving at school during any given year. Parents will not have to keep their children at home after they have attained school age merely because of an arbitrary rule set by the school board. Most important, children will stand a far better chance of being treated as persons, because they will not arrive at school in groups.

Nor will they be processed through twelve years of school the same way. For when a student completes Grade One he moves on to Grade Two. And if he began Grade One on March 10, he will complete Grade One on March 10 the following year—and move to Grade Two. The point, of course, is this: If we have to live with a system of school that carves education into twelve year-long slices called *grades,* is it unreasonable to ask that each child move through the grades as a person and not as a member of a group—especially since schools talk so much about individualized learning? Is this not common sense?

This plan is at once practical and subversive. It is practical, because obviously it can be made to work, if the school wants to make it work.* Nothing about it is complicated, and much about it is attractive. Under this plan, no more than perhaps three or four new students would arrive in a given class each month, and rarely more than one new student on any one day. The teacher thus has the opportunity to get to know his or her students as the individuals they are. At the early grade levels, where security and feeling at home are particularly important to a child, the teacher can devote time to the new arrival—to welcome the youngster and begin to determine his or her needs. Children who have been in the class for a time and know their way around the classroom and are familiar with the daily routines can help each newcomer to get acclimated. The experience of mutual assistance, one child for another, is helpful in building a sense of compassion and concern for others, qualities much needed in today's society. Each newcomer can be welcomed by a brief birthday celebration—songs, dances and games—to help make a warm beginning for the new child, and to be a constructive learning experience for the group as a whole. At the higher grades— high school, for example—the advantages are comparable: Because the student arrives at each grade level as a person, the chances are far greater that he or she will be dealt with as a person, and the opportunities for making education a personal experience are enhanced.

The subversive power of the birthday policy is its capacity to disrupt many of the standard, unquestioned practices of schools —practices that lend to school much of its stiff, inflexible character. With students moving from grade level to grade level on their birthdays at various days and times of the year, the basic group processing system is disrupted. In any given grade, though

* The Teaneck, New Jersey, public schools tried this plan several years ago, when Harvey Scribner was superintendent of schools there. The plan was recommended by Scribner and was supported enthusiastically by a majority of the Teaneck Board of Education. After Scribner left Teaneck, the plan was abandoned. There are differing explanations of why the plan was dropped, but one reason, it seems clear, was the inability of administrators to prepare teachers to treat students as persons instead of as "classes" or "grades." There also was an expressed concern that the birthday plan would spoil the high-school graduation ceremony twelve years later, because students would complete their high-school work on different days.

all the students are in the same grade—Grade Two, say, or Grade Five—there will be few students who will have been in the grade the same length of time, and few will graduate from that grade on exactly the same day. Each student will proceed on a personal schedule—and the teacher, therefore, will have to work out learning schedules that are personal to each child. There is room for group activities, to be sure, as well as for youngsters working in pairs and small groups. But, because of the unique arrival and departure times of each student, the teacher will find it virtually impossible to take the entire group page by page through the math book, the history book, or the reading series.

Schools constantly claim that they cater to individual students. This plan would help make the rhetoric operational. Each child necessarily would have to have his own plan or program for learning—his own folder for math work, for example, and his own record of reading progress. A standardized program would be almost impossible to operate. Each child's progress would be a measure of his own advancement—what he can do today as compared with last week or last month. Comparisons with other children would be irrelevant, since no two began the grade at the same time and they are not working on the same lessons. Each child of necessity will have to be given work at his own level and ability, and each will have to be allowed to proceed at his own rate. Each child will have to be helped individually. Group instruction, for most purposes, will be impractical. One child's strengths can be used to help fellow students with their weaknesses, with his weaknesses helped in turn. With this simple policy honestly applied, the factory assembly-line technique will be destroyed.

How much more will it cost? The cost of putting this idea into practice is no more per child than keeping the present system going. There will be an increased enrollment of children the first year the plan is used at the level of Grade One or Kindergarten, because some children will be eligible sooner for school than under the conventional policy. But the enrollment increase occurs only the first year of the plan. Thereafter, the only noticeable change will be the first-year enrollment "bulge" moving upward one year at a time through the school system, until the "extra" children—who really are not extras at all—who comprise the bulge are graduated from high school. While this may cause temporary budgetary increases at each grade level, the school district in the long run educates no more children than it otherwise would; it simply enrolls them differently.

Let's look, for example, at a school district that has 100 children in its kindergarten and decides to adopt the birthday policy. Since the district produces 100 five-year-olds each year, the arithmetic works out to a statistical average of 8.3 birthdays each month. Let's say the policy takes effect at the beginning of a school year in September. Since the district typically registers 100 five-year-olds each September, we must assume 100 five-year-olds will register in September when the birthday policy begins. But under the birthday policy, other children will arrive after September as each reaches his fifth birthday. Based on the statistical average of 8.3 birthdays a month, we can project the approximate kindergarten enrollment for Year One as follows: 100 children when school opens in September; 108 by September 30; 117 by October 30; 125 by November 30; 133 by December 30; 141 by January 30; 150 by February 28; 158 by March 30; 166 by April 30, and 175 by May 30. The number of new children in June will depend on the cut-off date of the policy and the day school closes. Children with birthdays in the summer months will enter kindergarten the following September.

In Year Two of the plan, kindergarten enrollment will return over the course of the year to its normal level. At the same time, the first-year bulge will move up to Grade One. Each year thereafter, the bulge will move up again. In a school district where enrollments are stable, the bulge will represent about a 5 to 7 percent increase in students, but it affects only one grade level at a time. The problem should not cause a good school administrator to lose sleep. He can enlist assistance from a university that is interested in school reform, that is willing to send prospective teachers to the district as part of their teacher training, or that is willing to encourage its students to go to the district as volunteer tutors. Paraprofessionals and teacher assistants can be hired to help with the added children at the affected grade level. Ideally, the district can put the policy into effect at a time when statistical projections show a decrease in kindergarten enrollments, a situation not uncommon these days in many communities. With imagination, the district can use its own high-school students to help as tutors and teacher assistants in the lower grades, thereby allowing the district to deal with the kindergarten "bulge" without hiring more teachers for a one-year administrative problem.

The basic point is this: The birthday plan does not require an extra dollar from the school district, because no child will get any more schooling than he gets without the plan. All that is required to implement it is administrative determination.

The administrator will have to offer genuine leadership. He will have to educate parents to the new policy, emphasizing its advantages to children. He will have to convince teachers that the policy is worthwhile, and that it will be applied in spite of complaints that may be heard.

And there will be complaints. For though the plan is simple, the implications are profound. Because it delivers students to school as persons, it makes it difficult for teachers and administrators to resist making substantial changes in the common practices of teaching to groups, testing groups, processing groups, and measuring student achievements against group norms and group standards.

The birthday plan is a small piece of dynamite in the standard practices of schools, and no perceptive professional will fail to see this. He'll see the challenge to the order, tradition and discipline of the institution, and he'll rise in objection. Hopefully, the cool-headed proponent of this plan will challenge the opponent with questions as simple as the plan itself: Do you believe schools should treat children as persons or as groups? Do you believe in individualized learning? What precisely are the administrative problems this policy will cause, and how serious are they? Are these problems so complicated that a staff of intelligent, hardworking professional educators cannot solve them? Will these problems mostly affect the adults in the schools or the children?

Finally: problems aside, does the idea look like a good thing for kids? If so, why not try it? Do schools exist to minimize the problems of its employees, or to maximize opportunities for the young?

/ *The Year-Round-Learning-Center Plan*

John Dewey said—and he is often quoted—that "education is not a preparation for life, it is life itself." Few school professionals would disagree; yet schools and their administrators tend, at least implicitly, to run schools as if they were quite separate and apart from the whole experience of life and growing up.

If education is to be life itself, it follows that becoming educated should be an integral part of living, and school should fit into the lives of students and their families—which is quite different from being imposed on their lives. There are proposals today to abolish compulsory schooling, or to lower the age at which the young legally may leave school. Apart from this issue, however, there is no reason that compulsory-school-attendance laws necessarily have to be applied as they presently are. There is room for a good deal of significant educational reform even with compulsory school laws—if schools apply the law imaginatively.

This plan is for transforming a ten-months-a-year school into a year-round learning center. This is more than another recommendation that schools be open twelve months a year for the sake of making maximum use of school buildings. This is a simple proposal to keep the school open all year round and let families, not the school, decide which days they wish their children to attend school, provided that they send them enough days to meet the requirements of the compulsory-attendance law.

A "learning center" might work like this:

A school district would designate one or several of its schools, either elementary or secondary, as year-round learning centers. All the district needs to do is direct the school in question to be open twelve months a year instead of the usual nine or ten months. It might well say that the learning center will be open for business on the same days as the post office, which is a handy rule for parents and children to remember.

The second thing the school district would do is say to the participating families: "Look, it is required by law and policy that every child attend school. In this district, the minimum number of school days is set at 180 days a year. This learning center will operate like any other school in the district, except that it will be open five days a week, twelve months a year, except for national holidays—a total of approximately 250 days. You decide which 180 days you want your child to go to school, and send him on those days. As long as your child attends school at least 180 days during the year, the requirements are met. If your child begins to attend school with insufficient regularity to meet this requirement, then state laws and local policies prevail, and the school district's responsibility will be the same as it is for any other school in the district: to enforce the compulsory-attendance law with all the means we have, including, if necessary, the courts."

Participation in the learning center, the school district would announce, will be voluntary. That is to say, conventional ten-month schools with the usual September-to-June schedule will continue to be available in the school district for those families that prefer them. The learning center will be open to all families, but only those who choose it will be involved. (Needless to say, if the school district wants the plan to succeed, the school-district leaders are responsible for telling parents of the advantages of the plan, and why their children should participate in it.)

It should be obvious that the plan is not a way of circumventing compulsory attendance in schools. Rather, it is a way of allowing families to fit school into their lives and their schedules, and thereby help to make the experience of going to school more a part of life. Where those in charge of a learning center feel that they must have some advance notice from parents as to which days they plan to send their children to school, so that forty children won't show up the same morning to work with a teacher who has only thirty places in his classroom, the center may ask parents a week or so in advance to select their preferred days on a first-come-first-served basis.

The rationale for this plan consists of two parts. First, with regard to having schools open all year round, since public schools are public agencies providing educational services, it makes no sense to shut down these agencies and shut off their services for two or more months every year. We would consider it absurd to close the public library two or three months a year—or the public roads, or the public sanitation system or city hall. Yet we do it with schools in the name of tradition, and justify it on the ground that "parents won't have it any other way." Parents, of course, have been trained to think of schools as ten-month operations, because that's what they always have been. Moreover, parents have never really been offered a constructive, interesting alternative; the typical plan for year-round schools merely takes the old ten-month school and keeps it running an additional two months. Under the typical year-round school plan, no one promises that the experience of going to school will be different for children. No one says to the parent, "Look, under this plan, you've got some choices that you haven't had before." Generally, the idea of year-round schools is an economic argument. This plan for year-round learning centers is an educational proposal—a reform idea.

The second part of the rationale concerns compulsory school attendance. Virtually every state by law requires school-age children and youth to attend school. Typically, schools are open approximately 180 days a year, and the law says school-age children have to be in school on those days unless properly excused. This plan does not ask that compulsory-attendance laws be repealed or that their powers be diminished in any way. (We are not convinced by the arguments to abolish compulsory schooling. In our view, it is not enough to repeal the laws or lower the age at which children may leave school legally. There has to be a constructive alternative to school—a place to go, opportunities to be had. Right or wrong, this society continues to place a heavy emphasis on education, diplomas and degrees, and until alternatives to school come into view, abolishing the compulsory-attendance laws may do more to empower schools to rid themselves of "disruptive" children and "slow learners" than to free the young.) This plan, in short, is based not on abolishing compulsory attendance, but on allowing the student and his family to meet the demands of the law in a wholly different way. If the state has the right to command the young to go to school for their own educational good, should not the young (and their families) at least have the right to choose the days that are most convenient for them? The family thus obtains a new dimension of choice and responsibility. The student thus becomes, at least in part, a volunteer student; each day he is in school he knows that he does not have to be there, for he could come another day instead. Parents exercising responsibility; students in school by choice—aren't these conditions in keeping with the purposes of schools? Aren't they part of education?

This plan admittedly raises some problems, but they are not insurmountable. Some teachers and administrators would be needed on a year-round basis, and school buildings would have to be kept open all year round, which means that there would be some additional operating and maintenance costs. It might even be necessary in some parts of the country to install air conditioning to keep school buildings comfortable during warm weather. But putting school teachers on twelve-month contracts is neither unusual nor undesirable. And look at what happens now: buildings that cost millions of dollars stand idle for weeks at a time; trained teachers are left to work at summer jobs (or are left unemployed) for a quarter of each year; and families are told to send their children to school on a particular set of days between September and June with no regard for the convenience of the parents or children involved.

The problems raised do not make this plan impractical; they simply make it necessary to run schools differently. The school district in any event will not be educating any additional children, or educating any children for extra days. In order to prevent extra costs that would result if a family chose to send a child to school more than 180 days, the district if it wishes can limit the number of days a child can come to school in a given year to the 180 days that are required.

The advantages of this plan are numerous. Families can weigh their own schedules and plans, and fit school to them. When a boy or girl has the chance to go fishing with his or her father or on a trip with his or her parents, who can say that this is less educational than being in school one day? Working parents have their own schedules to keep, and many parents do not have days off that coincide with school vacations; think of the advantages to them if they could choose the days to send their children to school. Other families prefer winter vacations: why shouldn't they be able to take their children with them, as long as the youngsters attend school during another part of the year? Closing schools during the summer months goes back to the days when most families were farmers, and the children were needed to work on the farm in the summer. To maintain a traditional school calendar when most families live in cities or in suburbs makes no sense, especially when beneficial reform would be so simple.

There are other advantages, too. The parents' responsibility to select the school days is consistent with the need to bring parents closer to educational decisions. A student's illness no longer would require an "excuse"; he simply goes to school another day. Costly school buildings would be used more; it is reasonable to expect that a school that accommodates 1,000 children on a ten-month year could accommodate 1,200 if used twelve months (a 20 percent increase). The implication, of course, is that we would need fewer new schools or additions to existing schools. The teaching staff of a school could be augmented during the summer months with college students (potential tutors and teacher assistants), vacationing adult residents of the community (potential teachers of special skills and crafts, such as carpentry, creative writing, home buying, and so on), as well as teachers from school districts that have yet to adopt twelve-month school calendars. Some teachers could be hired on twelve-month contracts, others on conventional ten-month contracts, and still others, by mutual consent, on six-month or short-term contracts.

If the school district finds it unnecessary to limit the number of days on which a child can come to school, the youngster who wishes to accelerate his education has the chance to do so by attending extra days, and the student who wishes to make up some work he has not yet passed can do that. Finally, the school district—because it will be doing something few other districts have done—has the chance to attract the attention of a university that is interested in school reform. If it is a university that trains teachers, there is the possibility of negotiating a collaborative agreement for teacher training.

Most important, because the standard school calendar would be broken, children no longer would arrive and leave in groups, and therefore assembly-line practices and group instruction would be undermined. Like the birthday-entrance plan, the plan for a year-round learning center is innocent in appearance but highly subversive in its potential impact. Where children now can be marched through school in groups because they all have to come to school on the same days, this plan would make it hard on the school to keep this up, because the school would no longer know what particular days a particular child would be coming to school. Each child would have, in effect, his own school calendar; and he, not the school, would set it. Each child would have to be dealt with as a person; he would have to have his own program, and he would have to work through it at his own rate and in keeping with his own ability. His progress would have to be a measure of his own rate of advancement—since there could be no such constant as a "class" that begins in September and ends in June. The school, in short, would find it difficult *not* to become a learning center to which individual children would come to work on their individual programs of learning on days that they, the learners, had chosen.

The target of this simple idea is the lockstep of schooling. The device that makes the idea work is having families select the days a child goes to school. As with the birthday-entrance plan, as soon as the students are delivered to school in a different way—specifically, as individuals—the group-processing system of school is exposed and disrupted. Where families choose the school days for their children, the school cannot organize classes in quite the same way, since the members of any "class" would not be in school on the same days consistently. Learning, by definition, would have to begin where the child left off—not where the group is. Teachers would be forced to assess and alter most time-worn practices and procedures. Instruction would have to be individualized, since there is no realistic alternative when the presence of unchanging groups of students cannot be required on a daily basis. Classes, classrooms, class instruction, bells and schedules would no longer serve as administrative procedures for assorting, labeling and distributing students to their stations: such devices in fact would disrupt a "learning center," and therefore would have to be abandoned. Roles and responsibilities of learners and teachers would have to be reviewed and redefined. The school staff would have to make it feasible for the individual youngster to plug into a suitable program.

The year-round learning center does not propose to save a community money. And it is guaranteed to cause headaches for those who manage schools and teach in schools. But that is part of the purpose: to make the people who control schools question what they are doing and to change much of what they do. It is not that the people who control schools are bad people who deliberately do bad things to children. Rather, it is that most of them have talked themselves into believing that they treat children as persons, whereas in fact they process them as groups. We have no desire to make life hard for teachers and school administrators. But we do believe that schools ought to make life better for students and parents, and that going to school ought to be a part of life, not separate from it.

If having good teachers and keeping them is as important to the education of children as most people say it is, there ought to be a way of paying the very best teachers as much as, or more than, a principal. Common sense should tell us this. The common practice, however, is not to do it.

The typical way of paying teachers has nothing directly to do with their on-the-job performance or their demonstrated success with children.* In most school districts, teachers are paid according to a set pay scale, which is negotiated by organized teachers and the school district. A teacher's salary is determined on the scale by the number of years he or she has been a teacher and the highest college degree the teacher has earned. It's a

---

* Much the same can be said of the typical system by which teachers are licensed by the state. Typically, the license-granting apparatus rests for the most part on university courses taken and successfully completed—not on demonstrated competence on the job. The point here is not to criticize the quality or usefulness of university programs that train teachers (though there is plenty of room for criticism). Nor is it to suggest that university training ought to have no connection with the licensing of teachers; no doubt there should continue to be some connection between the two. The point is that it is ludicrous for teachers to hold their licenses aloft, as many of them often do, as if they are documentary proof of professional competence; clearly, they are not. Licenses are merely the public's written permission to practice a profession—and therefore the public has both the right and the responsibility to review the holders of its licenses periodically to ensure that the holders continue to meet minimum requirements. This point, concerning periodic review and renewal of licenses, is found objectionable by many teachers, who seem to think that licenses ought to be good for a lifetime. Such a view ignores the fundamental purpose of a teaching license—to protect children, whom the law compels to go to school, from inferior teachers.

classic civil-service system in which the variables that determine salary level are longevity (years of teaching service) and academic training (degrees held or credits earned). A teacher thus earns more the longer he teaches. Similarly, the teacher with a Ph.D. earns more than one with a master's degree, and the latter in turn earns more than a colleague with only a B.A.

It might be assumed that teachers would object to this kind of rigid, antiperformance system, especially those teachers who know in their bones that they are more skillful in their craft than most teachers and therefore really deserve higher compensation. Teachers, like any professionals, want the opportunity to earn higher salaries, and it is as plain to them as it is to anyone else that teachers are not equal in ability or commitment, and to pay them as if they were is irrational. Teachers know, too, that the conventional salary system, based as it is on factors that do not reflect performance, tends to reward and protect mediocre and inferior teachers, discourages the most creative and most successful teachers and, worst of all perhaps, drives many of the best teachers out of teaching and into supervisory or administrative jobs as the means of obtaining a higher salary.

But teachers on the whole not only do not object to the conventional salary system; they and their organizations work hard to keep it in use. More important to teachers than the obvious flaws and shortcomings in the conventional salary system is their fear that it would be replaced by "merit pay," the perennial alternative to traditional salary scales. In general, teachers oppose merit pay because they distrust the idea that someone will decide which teachers are worthy of merit salary increases—which means that all teachers somehow will have to be evaluated and measured. If there is anything that scares most teachers it is the prospect of having their performance assessed, even where a positive finding could result in more pay. What criteria would be used to evaluate teachers? Who would set the criteria? Who would decide which teachers would get more pay? Would teachers who do not get merit pay be able to appeal? What would guarantee against biased decisions? What would happen to teacher morale if teachers received different salaries?

The opposition of teachers to merit-pay proposals has been consistently strong; and merit pay, as the result, is a dead issue. Why, teachers ask, should their salaries be subjected to the whim of a principal or other school administrator, whose personal opinion of a teacher's performance would be the cornerstone of a merit-pay system? (The question reflects the teacher's inherent belief that a principal's role is to keep a building open and running smoothly, not make hard decisions about the quality of teachers. Further, most teachers believe principals don't have the capacity or ability to evaluate teachers.)

Merit pay is a topic that seems forever to be discussed at conferences and conventions, and never to be adopted. But this should not deter parents from pursuing new ways of paying teachers that will result ultimately in better teachers for children. After all, one thing that cannot be said of the conventional salary-scale method of paying teachers is that it serves the educational interest of the young. Clearly, it has nothing whatever to do with the needs of children—or even with education. It is a bureaucratic scheme of, by and for the working school professional, and anything done to replace it with policies that relate a teacher's salary directly to his performance would constitute a notable educational reform.

There may be a way to begin to do this without resurrecting the ghost of merit pay. We call it The Most-Wanted-Teacher Plan—or how to pay a teacher more than a principal. This plan is based on the simple premise that it is in the public's interest (and the interest of children) that the most successful teachers be rewarded financially, because they then are more likely to keep on teaching; and that parents be empowered to choose the teachers they want for their children, because this choice is basic to closer parental involvement in school affairs and greater parental responsibility for the education of children as well.

This plan, therefore, calls for parents to select teachers for their children, and for teachers to be paid in keeping with the number of children each attracts. The more students who sign with a teacher, the higher the teacher's pay. The extra pay is not merit pay, because no one has officially made an evaluation of the teacher's performance and no official body has made a decision as to whether the teacher does or does not deserve a salary increase. What a teacher earns is a direct reflection of how many students (and their parents) he can satisfy; nothing more. In the absence of any better, agreed-upon performance criteria—and with a view toward empowering parents to take more direct control and responsibility for their own schools—what could be more reasonable? How could a line of accountability be drawn more distinctly and directly between teachers and parents?

A Most-Wanted-Teacher Plan might work like this:

A school district, by adoption of a policy in public meeting after full public discussion, would declare that beginning in a specified school year parents of children in the primary or elementary grades would select their children's teachers.*

The district would set up methods for informing parents in detail about the teachers available, as well as their teaching styles. The information should include basic advice as to what to look for in a classroom, the elements of a classroom environment that contribute to (and inhibit) learning, how to match the learning needs and learning styles of children with the teaching styles of teachers, how to distinguish between the enjoyment of learning and sheer entertainment, and some pointers as to what constitutes becoming educated. This parent-education aspect of the plan is critical; if parents are to make decisions they have not had the opportunity to make before, they need some basic training and briefing. (It is interesting that automobile and boat manufacturers make abundant use of brochures, photographs, movies and, now, video cassette recorders to inform consumers about the details of their various sales lines. It has occurred to us that schools could do much the same thing to inform parents about teaching styles.) Parents, needless to say, should be afforded the chance to see teachers teaching and classrooms in operation be-

---

* A version of this plan no doubt could be adapted for secondary schools. Provisions, however, would have to be made to adjust for the departmentalized nature of high schools, and the practice of "required" and "elective" courses. Obviously, adjustments would be needed so that the teachers of required courses did not have undue advantages over the teachers of electives.

fore being asked to decide which teacher or teachers they want. Ultimately, in accordance with an established schedule, each family would choose teachers for their children. Provision should be made for reasonable changes during the year—a family clearly should be able to shift a child from one teacher to a second teacher where the first choice seemed not to work for the child. Families moving into the district during the school year would have the same rights to choose teachers as any other family.

The district, before the opening of the school year, would assign students to teachers in keeping with the parents' choices. The district by this time would have set two figures: the maximum number of children one teacher could serve before extra help is hired or the group of children is divided ("maximum class size" is the conventional term), and the smallest number of children that would constitute a class (this figure likely would be about half the "maximum-class-size" figure).

The district would count the number of children choosing each teacher and would compute teacher salaries accordingly. For example, if the "maximum class size" is set at 30 students, a teacher with 60 children would receive double his regular salary, a teacher with 90 would get triple salary, a teacher with 45 would receive an extra half salary, and so on. Depending on the details of the ground rules set by the district, teachers would receive pro rata salary increments for each student (or every three or every five) in excess of the "maximum-class-size" figure.

The teacher would use all or part of his extra income to buy the services of extra teachers, teacher assistants, aides, and so on, who the teacher feels are needed and are appropriate for the children in his or her charge. In general, the teacher would have to buy as many extra services and different kinds of services as are needed to retain his or her students. The method used to buy services and employ assistance, whether teachers or aides or classroom supplies, would be spelled out in the ground rules set by the school district. The rules, obviously, should be fair to teachers and parents alike, and consistent with law and sound business policy.

Teachers chosen by at least the minimal number of students

required to constitute a class but not more than the "maximum-class-size" number would receive a normal salary. A teacher chosen by fewer than the minimum needed for a class would be, in effect, a teacher without students. He or she might be hired by a most-wanted teacher who is "employing" extra help to serve his students. Or the teacher without students might be desired in another school in the district, in which case that teacher might be reassigned. Ultimately, if no place can be found for such a teacher in the school district—which means his or her services are not requested by a sufficient number of students—the teacher's job would be abolished, and the teacher dismissed. A dismissal of this kind no doubt would lead to an appeal, and perhaps a court case.

It would be interesting to see how a court would rule where a school district can demonstrate with documentation and evidence that its teacher-choice plan was properly adopted by the school board, that the plan was the product of careful planning, that the plan has provisions to preclude unfairness and promote reasonableness, that the plan has been instituted and is operating successfully, and that the teacher had been dismissed only because his services could not be "sold" to a minimum number of families. One has to wonder whether a court would require the public to keep a teacher on its payroll under such circumstances.

This plan, surely, has some problem areas; no one could answer all the potential questions such a plan would raise until a detailed procedure was actually laid out and the plan had begun to operate. Frankly, we do not expect any school district to adopt such a plan; we know that there are many strong opponents to the idea of parents being empowered to choose teachers, and that teacher organizations are concerned about the job rights and pay scales of teachers.

But the idea is worth talking about—perhaps there is a school district somewhere that might be willing to try some version of it. For, with all the problems this plan might raise, it stands in favorable contrast to how students are matched with teachers now. Some schools make an attempt, however feeble, to match youngsters and teachers with regard for the needs and characteristics of the child. Most do not. A few provide for parent preferences; the great bulk of schools give no thought to it. The typical public school divides students among teachers like so many bodies—25 for Miss X, 25 for Mrs. Y, 25 for Mr. Z. In more than a few schools the assignment of students to teachers is more a clerical routine than a professional decision. So, when we talk about the idea of parents choosing teachers, let's not assume that, if implemented, it would destroy a rational, useful system that is doing something positive for children.

Wouldn't it be interesting for once to see a successful, creative —wanted—teacher have 100 children in his or her charge, and the equivalent of three extra salaries to use as the teacher sees fit? He might have one extra teacher, a couple of teacher assistants, some parent volunteers (the most-wanted-teacher could pay for their transportation and baby sitters), some out-of-school trips, extra magazines, newspapers and games, a few new books, perhaps a film, and so on. Wouldn't it be nice to see a most-wanted-teacher invest his extra funds in part-time helpers and short-term activities for the benefit of his students—a craftsman for a half-day a week, a reading specialist for two days a week, a creative-writing helper for three days a week, and so on? Wouldn't it be nice, for once, to have teachers with an authentic sense of being wanted by parents and a sense that they work for and are responsible to the parents of the children they teach?

Would those employed by the most-wanted-teachers be the employees of the school district? Perhaps; we would leave this to the desires of the school board, and the ground rules established for the plan; more complicated technical matters than this have been worked out by every school district of any size that has federal, state and local funds going into its programs. What about fringe benefits for the people the most-wanted-teachers employ? Any good business manager could handle this problem so that everyone pays his taxes and stays in the Social Security system. What about union contracts with teachers? This is a real problem, and hard negotiation surely would be necessary. But if newspapers can go to automation with the agreement of their printers, perhaps it's not so impossible for schools to negotiate their way through this, especially if parents support the idea.

Teachers have rights, and their rights deserve protection. But it should be remembered that parents also have rights, including the right to have something to say about their children's education, and that's what this plan is about. Children too have rights, including the right to have a teacher they want, and one who seems to want them. Are the rights of parents and students to be ignored because an idea designed to help children might temporarily disturb the job security of some adults?

The most-wanted-teacher idea will be fought—by parents who don't understand the purpose, don't want the responsibility that goes with it, or fear any kind of change; by teachers who view the plan as "unprofessional," who fear that parents' choosing of teachers will deteriorate into popularity contests, or who fear their own abilities will be misjudged; and by school superintendents and school-board members who don't want to take the risk of supporting such an idea in the face of strong opposition, though they know at first hand the inadequacies of the present ways of assigning children to teachers and the senselessness of paying all teachers alike.

What could be more open, more honest or fairer? Schools already grant extra pay for extra work—to football coaches, to the adviser of the student newspaper, to the teachers who teach night courses and summer courses in addition to their regular school-year teaching assignments. If a teacher is willing to be responsible for twice as many students as other teachers, shouldn't he or she be paid twice as much? Isn't the maxim, "equal pay for equal work," applicable to schools? If parents don't mind the fact that their teacher has extra students in his charge—after all, they chose him—why should anyone else object? Is the teacher who has only twenty-five children harmed? Doesn't he have the same opportunity to attract extra students? Is any child hurt by this plan? As long as the teacher is paid on the basis of objective facts—how many kids he or she teaches—and not on the basis of a subjective judgment of his or her teaching ability, do the old arguments against merit pay apply? As long as the school district pledges that the plan will not result in extra costs—that extra compensation for most-wanted teachers will be offset by teachers dismissed for lack of students—will the taxpayer (who also is the parent) object?

Schools are always talking about the gulf between education and the home, and about the "bridges" that are needed to bring about more effective education. This is a bridge. They're also constantly talking about accountability—school to parent, teacher to child. This is basic accountability. Teachers are fond of talking about the paradox that you have to leave teaching for administration to get a pay increase. This speaks directly to the issue. For all the potential problems this idea may raise, it ought to have the support of all the people who say that they are concerned with bridges between home and school, with accountability, and with keeping good teachers teaching.

PLAN IV / *The Apprenticed-Learner Plan*

This proposal is short, simple and subversive. Its object is to raise the educational opportunities of some high-school students by getting them out of school—not as dropouts, but as out-of-school students.

The plan is based on premises that few would contest. The first is one that every trained teacher has heard at one time or another: Learning by doing is an effective and time-proven way of learning. The second is that one tends to learn best when the material or skill to be learned is of real interest to the learner; we learn quickly and well what we want or need to learn. The third premise is that there are in the world many more teachers than just those who are in the teaching profession. In a very real sense, we are all teachers of a sort—parents teach their children language and culture; employers teach their employees work skills; neighbors and friends teach one another various avocational skills and hobbies; we teach one another to sew, to repair home appliances and to drive automobiles. Few individuals go through life without having taught something to someone, whether or not they were conscious of their teaching role. The final point is that any number of students of high-school age—in the "best" high schools as well as in the worst; with high IQ's and with low IQ's—find school dull. Therefore, they achieve at a lower level than if they were interested; and thus, too, they acquire a personal distaste for learning, associating it, on the basis of their own experience, with boredom and pain. This is the wastefulness of the high-school experience of many young people.

The Apprenticed-Learner Plan would do this:

1. It would have the school—a high school—comb the citizen rolls of the town or city to which it belongs, and identify the most reputable, skilled professionals and craftsmen. The preliminary list would be as long and inclusive as possible: artists, musicians, researchers, cabinetmakers, technicians, scientists, doctors, dentists, salesmen, builders, designers, architects, accountants, attorneys, et cetera. From this list, the school would prepare a list of working or retired artisans, artists, professionals and craftsmen who (a) possess a skill worth teaching; (b) have good reputations in their fields; and (c) are willing to teach their craft to a high-shool student on an apprenticeship basis.

2. The school, from its list, would select appropriate nonschool instructors and would assign to them students who have enlisted in the apprenticed-learner program. The school will have to devise a system for determining eligibility, but whatever the system, each apprenticeship arrangement would have the approval of the student, the parents, the nonschool instructor and the school, to guarantee the voluntary participation of student and instructor and to ensure the proper support. Apprenticeships would be based on written contracts—a standard form could be drawn up by the school. Each contract should specify, in general terms, the parameters of the apprenticeship, which is to say the resources that the apprenticeship instructor agrees to provide, the duration of the apprenticeship, the resources the school will offer, and the kind of experience the student will gain. An apprenticeship may be as short as one semester or longer than a school year. For the duration of the apprenticeship the student would work full time with the instructor while the student remains enrolled in school and participates like any other student in extracurricular and after-school activities, visits periodically with the school advisers and participates every week or two in a seminar in which apprenticed learners may share their experiences and problems.

3. When the student has successfully completed his or her apprenticeship and the fact is certified by the instructor, the student would be granted academic credit for the apprenticeship

period. The instructor would be paid a stipend based on the school's per-student spending and the amount of instructional time that the apprenticeship consumed. In addition to the work associated with the apprenticeship, the school may assign the student work in more conventional subject-matter areas, such as English and history, on an independent-study basis. Further, the student may be required to demonstrate his or her competence in the skills acquired through the apprenticeship, as a condition for receiving credit.

Though few will contest the simple premises on which this plan rests, many will loudly object to the plan itself. Some professional teachers will say that the proposal is scandalous and unprofessional because it would place students in the hands of untrained teachers. "Quackery," someone is likely to say. (Perhaps some people fear that the public will discover that there is more than one way to educate, and that we don't necessarily need a trained teacher every step along the path, and that some of the best teaching is available from people who are not professional teachers.)

Some principals and other school administrators will suggest that the proposal is unworkable. Students, one hears, will be out of sight of the school and in the charge of people who are not school employees. And who, for heaven's sake, will be responsible for taking their attendance? (Perhaps what concerns such administrators is that they will have to devise more than one administrative way to keep track of students, and that they will have to invent some realistic methods for measuring what a student knows, so that credits can be granted and diplomas issued.)

Someone will reject the concept as impractical, because the state, "as everyone knows," won't allow unlicensed teachers to practice education. But the plan would keep the student enrolled in school, and legally in the care of licensed school professionals. State departments of education, which issue teacher licenses, are increasingly open to new ideas in the certification and licensing of teachers, particularly ideas related to performance-based licensing. It is fair to assume, therefore, that a licensing agency that is inclined toward administrative experimentation is not likely to put up roadblocks if a school makes a persuasive case for an experiment of its own.*

And one can foresee a taxpayer objection: What right does the school have to pay public funds to these individuals who will do the instructing? What right does the school have to pay public funds to such individual entrepreneurs as architects and writers and artists? Is this not a subsidy?

And, finally, how do we know that this innovation would work? The answer to this has got to be a straightforward: "We don't." But neither do we know, when any given student enters high school, that any ordinary high-school program will "work" for him or her. The only thing we *do* know is that our regular schools do *not* succeed with every student.

If the students who sign up do so voluntarily and with the permission of parents and school; if their education for the time they work as apprenticed learners does not cost the public any more than if they simply went to classes at school; if the state department of education does not mind and the local school board has no objections—what's to be lost by trying? Should the objections of teachers cause the plan to be rejected? If the principal objects, is this reason enough not to pursue it? If guidance counselors are cool to the idea, should parents and students who wish to try something new for themselves—and on themselves—be denied the right to do it?

The real advantage of apprenticed learning is not the teaching

---

* It is worth noting that the vast majority of the apprenticeship instructors are "licensed" already—by their profession, by the state, and in some cases by both. While this is not a license to teach, it is official certification of competence to practice in their respective fields. We are not in any sense suggesting that a license in one field constitutes authority to practice in any field; a teaching license does not authorize the holder to practice dentistry or medicine or law. But it is absurd, on the other hand, to contend that a trained attorney, licensed to practice in his field, is barred from helping a public-school student who comes to the attorney's door of his own volition, and with his parent's and school's permission, to acquire some knowledge of law and some comprehension of how a lawyer works, simply because the attorney does not hold a teaching license. In brief, the notion of apprenticed learners does not make artists and professionals full-time teachers; it makes them added educational resources for students, to be tapped by students as part of their formal education.

of specific crafts and arts to the young; the purpose is not to produce junior-level professionals as Detroit turns out automobiles. The advantages are that the student learns that there are real connections between school and work, between acquiring an education and earning a living. He or she sees that education is practical. The gap between generations is narrowed to the extent that the young and their elders can see each other as individuals instead of abstractions; the role of the school as a broker of educational opportunity (instead of repository of knowledge) is demonstrated, and the term "teacher" is effectively redefined as "one who teaches" rather than as "one who holds a license to teach." The success or failure of the Apprenticed-Learner Plan is not to be measured simply by the quantitative evaluation of the skills acquired by the student in architecture or law or laboratory research or mechanics or carpentry or whatever. The measurement must include an assessment, however subjective, as to whether the students emerge from their apprenticeships with an expanded understanding of life and work, and with a sharpened desire to learn more about both.

It may be that in some states the plan cannot legally be tried without passage by the state legislature of enabling legislation. Such legislation, however, need not be elaborate; and requesting it could be as simple as the recommendation received by the Board of Education of the City of New York late in 1972:

[The New York City Board of Education should seek] passage of legislation which would allow the placing of volunteer students in individualized apprentice-style educational programs of specified duration and in cooperation with school authorities, with professionals, artists and craftsmen approved by a board of education, and to allow the payment of stipends to such professionals, artists and craftsmen for their instructional services.

The Board did not act on the recommendation.* If it had done so, it might have been the first school board in the nation to pursue, on a systematic basis, the creation of working apprenticeships for high-school students.

* The recommendation was made by Harvey Scribner, then Chancellor of the city school system, on the advice of staff, including Leonard Stevens.

PLAN V / *The Universal-Tutor Plan*

This plan is uncomplicated. It can be described most succinctly not by telling how it would work—because it could and should assume an infinite number of forms and shapes—but by describing what it would do if applied broadly to public education. It would provide each student, from the earliest levels of schooling through the high-school years, with an older student as a personal tutor. Every student in the public-education enterprise, beginning with adolescent years and continuing higher to include undergraduate students in publicly supported community colleges, four-year colleges and universities, would serve as a tutor to a younger colleague. Thus, every student, for the great majority of his formal schooling, would gain experience in the act of teaching.

The potential impact of this plan is enormous. The dollar cost is close to nil. There are obvious advantages in people-to-people understanding and public service, and few if any legal barriers. Research clearly shows the positive impact of students serving one another; it is familiar to practitioners and administrators at all levels of education.* Yet, comparatively few school districts have adopted the notion of youth teaching youth on any significant scale or made it an integral part of their programs. Although the number of such programs is increasing, at the present rate of adoption, the vast majority of the millions of students now in

* *Children Teach Children: Learning by Teaching,* by Alan Gartner, Mary Kohler, and Frank Riessman, is especially informative, including its bibliography, which cites much of the research in this field.

school will pass through the system without the benefits that tutoring can yield on both sides.

The primary benefits go to the tutor. If you find this surprising, we advise you to read *Children Teach Children: Learning by Teaching.* The authors of this valuable book, Alan Gartner, Mary Kohler, Frank Riessman, are experienced workers in youth programs. Hear them:

> It has long been obvious that children learn from their peers, but a more significant observation is that *children learn more from teaching other children.* From this a major educational strategy follows: namely, that every child must be given the opportunity to play the teaching role, because it is through playing this role that he may really learn how to learn.

One example described by these authors is a youth-tutoring-youth project in an antipoverty program. Over a five-month stretch of tutoring in reading, the youngsters gained six months on an achievement scale, while their tutors gained 3.4 years. We cite this not to suggest that peer tutoring is a panacea. It is not; the authors of *Children Teach Children* themselves note that gains in reading achievement do not necessarily produce parallel gains in grades in subject-matter areas. We cite the example to make the point that peer tutoring should be woven into the fabric of education, primarily for the learning opportunities it gives the student-tutor, rather than for the lesser benefits derived by the tutored youngsters. To give students the chance to teach is to give them an additional opportunity to learn. Conversely, to deny students the chance to teach is to constrict their educational opportunity, though in a way we have seldom attempted to measure or even see.

Potential tutors are in every classroom: undergraduate students in public universities; high-school students; students below the high-school years yet of sufficient age that their experience is of value to students who are younger still.*

* We would submit, though, that it does not always have to be a case of older students tutoring younger ones. We recall a visit we made several years ago to an evening-school program in New York City. The program was de-

Think of the teaching resources that go untapped: thousands upon thousands of undergraduate students on state university campuses, each of them obtaining a higher education with the assistance of a public subsidy, direct (loan or scholarship assistance) or indirect (reduced fees and tuitions, thanks to public tax dollars that built and operate the public universities). Does the public not have the right to ask publicly subsidized students to serve as tutors in the public's schools? Given the ideals of many young Americans, their desire to improve the condition of humanity, would not the request likely be answered willingly by a majority of college students, especially if the universities granted, as they should, academic credit for public service rendered?

Think, too, of the high schools of America, filled with students yearning for the chance to be on their own, to do something other than be a student (which, at this point in their lives, is the only career they know). How many of them would leap at the opportunity to be set free of their classrooms for a regular period of time, however brief, and spend that time helping a fellow student? The time and service would translate into diploma credits, just as time spent in classrooms. What about the student in high school or junior high who does not read well, whose self-esteem is low, who has experienced little but failure in his school life? For him or her, the chance to tutor a younger student would represent the chance to succeed at something, to sense pride and feel of value—and perhaps, in addition, to learn to read a bit better by having taught this "mysterious" skill to someone else.

How could we begin? One prerequisite is a rather more sophisticated piece of administrative machinery designed to articulate the complex institutional and human arrangements that have to be made for a program of this size to begin and to function smoothly. The public universities would have to build into their degree requirements for undergraduates a period of tutoring

---

signed to bring basic skills—reading, arithmetic, English grammar—to out-of-school youth and young adults. The program was based in part on tutoring, and it often paired tutors with learners without regard to age. We saw sixteen-year-olds tutoring twenty-year-olds, and quite successfully.

service to the students of the public schools (or, as an alternative to tutoring, another kind of public service); and they would have to convince themselves that such services are as worthy of credit as academic studies. The schools, for their part, would have to see that peer tutoring is an important, an essential element in educational opportunity; to prize and support it as much as report cards, lesson plans, varsity football teams and high-school marching bands—because it too will require space, materials, training and perhaps some transportation. Teachers would have to welcome as valued participants in a common endeavor, not as threats to their status and professional role, the tutors who work with their students. And parents will have to see that their children can work with one another as part of their learning and growth. They will have to be honestly persuaded that peer tutoring in these times of educational problems and fiscal stringencies is not a euphemism for watered-down education, a gimmick to be tried on the urban poor to save on teachers. The other prerequisite, in addition to administrative machinery, is more elusive —a critical but determined commitment by visionary school leaders to convince parents and professionals that peer tutoring is worth doing.

The poor, for good reasons, are wary and distrustful of school reform; calling for reform often looks like one more excuse for the failure to educate. One learns to be suspicious when one has been victimized over a long stretch of time. If you are poor, you tend to wonder why—now, when money is tight—the schools are suddenly saying that your kids would learn more if they tutored other kids and were tutored by them, instead of being taught by a university-trained teacher with a master's degree and five years' experience. "All I want for my children is what the others got— good teachers." Like all parents, poor parents have listened to the schools and heard that the best way to learn is at the foot of a trained teacher. It is difficult now to convince parents that that is not necessarily so. But the effort has to begin, and the sooner it does, the quicker there will be working, practical examples to point to.

PLAN VI / *The Zero-Construction Building Plan*

There is in western Massachusetts a country village with which we are each familiar. The population pattern is quite stable. There is no housing boom in progress and none on the immediate horizon, the numbers of children in the local schools are neither overwhelming nor accelerating markedly, and the school buildings on the whole are in better-than-average physical condition. There is no need, therefore, to build a new school to handle overcrowding or to meet a projected increase in enrollment, or to replace antiquated buildings. But if the school population were rising dramatically, or if one of the schools were in bad physical shape, it is not unreasonable to assume that there would be talk of school construction in this village. How do most communities solve such problems? They float a bond issue, buy some land, clear it, and construct a new school. And they do so without giving more than passing consideration to the alternative of finding the needed space in an existing building. At one end of town there is a church. Across the street from the church is a public library. And across from the library, there is a large restaurant. Next door to that building, are two good-sized meeting houses which belong to two local community organizations. As you go down the main road a few miles, there are more churches, a large, mostly empty factory, which has recently come to house an occupational-training program for handicapped people. There are also houses up for sale or rent, as well as business establishments that might be available in whole or in part for a modest price. Why don't we think of these spaces as potential learning space? What does it matter that they have never been used for education before, or that school-system administrations have generally, until recently, assumed that the only proper schoolhouses were those that were specially constructed as such?

The people of this village are as imaginative as any other set of Americans; and as taxpayers—because they are New Englanders and because their community cannot be described as rich or near-rich—they are probably more aware of the virtue of thrift in public spending than are their counterparts in many other communities. But they have been trained to build schools and have been taught that a school is a building, preferably large and identifiable as a school, and usually of red brick. Where else would modern children get their formal education but in a "big red schoolhouse"? Obviously, they could go to school in almost any kind of building, as long as it is clean, warm, comfortable and safe—and perhaps, for a number of reasons, be better off than in the enormous schools that we build for them. Not the least of it is that a school in a house or store would be smaller, the children would stand a better chance of standing out as individuals, of being known by their first name by the other children and the adults. This sense of belonging and of being known is something that ought not to be overlooked, especially for the youngest children. When young people complain of impersonality, when high-school students in big urban schools and university students on sprawling state campuses say that they feel like I.B.M. cards ("do not bend, fold or mutilate"), what they are really yearning for is a human-size place to learn in. When he was in New York City, Harvey Scribner asked for concrete solutions to violence and tension in high schools—a terrifying problem for urban schools everywhere—and one recommendation that came back to him repeatedly was to break up the enormous high schools, reorganize them internally so that the students would feel less alienated from their teachers and from one another, and to emphasize small schools in future planning.

We recommend a zero-construction building program to the

school districts of America. It is a simple plan. The school board would merely ask its chief administrator to draft a policy of constructing new school buildings only as a last resort, and searching first for existing space when additional space is needed. The school board, considering the policy, would hold public hearings, and following full discussion of the policy and its ramifications, hopefully adopt it. The district would be out of the school construction business, except for those rare instances when the administrators can prove to the school board's satisfaction that there is absolutely no alternative, not a square foot of space anywhere that could be successfully transformed into learning space. Where the school board or the administration drags its feet, or opposes such a policy, parents might bring the issue to public view, and lobby for it.

Where shall we find all this space that could be turned into schools? It is everywhere—right in front of our eyes, just as in the Massachusetts village. Probably every school district in America has some such space within its boundaries. Educational Facilities Laboratories calls it "found" space. E.F.L. is a small, exciting spin-off of the Ford Foundation, and in its own quiet, unrevolutionary way, it has in its short life contributed much to American students of all ages. E.F.L.'s mission is to "help schools and colleges with their physical problems by the encouragement of research and experimentation, and the dissemination of knowledge regarding educational facilities." It has thrown its prestige and grant money around the education enterprise in a conscious effort to replace the edifice complex of school administrators and school-board members with sensible planning. Found space, E.F.L. says, is "space a school system did not realize was there." It might even be space that the school district has overlooked in its own buildings, or is not using efficiently—such as large corridors and school lobbies, or inefficiently used auditoriums and cafeterias. But even more exciting than the potential usable space in crannies and caverns in school buildings is the "space lying close at hand in warehouses, factories, industrial plants, or in underused public buildings."

E.F.L. tells of these developments:

The City of Boston, having neither land, time nor money for a new school building, took half of an underused public bathhouse and renovated it into a 60,000-square-foot high-school annex. The modernization was accomplished during a summer. . . . A huge, cavernous locker room was converted into sixteen classrooms and a 90-by-110-foot gym. A cafetorium converts from four classrooms by opening operable walls. . . . The cost per student for a 450-student enrollment was about $1,450. . . .

An open classroom spin-off from Berkeley High School [in California] . . . expecting one hundred more students . . . needed flexible open plan space in a hurry. It settled on 5,000 square feet of vacant office space in an industrial building. The space was available on a short-term basis and could be had rent-free for a year in exchange for remodeling, with $1,500 per month rent thereafter. . . . The total cost for renovation was $13,000—$130 per student, or about $2.50 per square foot.

In New York City, P.S. 211 : . . has been successfully housed in a converted factory. . . . The lease is for fifteen years. . . .

The Philadelphia Board of Education has successfully converted several old buildings, including a supermarket, a warehouse-loft building, and a former arsenal, to school use. All the buildings were purchased, except the arsenal, which was a gift from the federal government. The school department has consistently found conversion costs to be lower than new construction costs. . . .

The Chicago School Department . . . modernized a fifty-year-old factory and its adjoining offices . . . bought a wholesale grocery warehouse and garage for $1 . . . [converted] a former candy factory [into learning space].*

The New York City school system spends millions of dollars on the renting, leasing and purchasing of all sorts of buildings: a catering hall, a theater, a bowling alley, an old newspaper plant. A "free" school we visited in central Manhattan was housed, quite comfortably, in a brownstone. Harlem Prep, an independent school that did notably good work with youngsters who had dropped out of regular schools and which, for reasons of diminishing economic support, recently was absorbed by the

* From *Schools: More Space / Less Money*, a report by Educational Facilities Laboratories.

New York City public-school system, was handsomely housed in a converted supermarket.

Are some of these schools likely to move out of these converted spaces as easily as they moved in? Perhaps. This is one of the advantages of leasing space, rather than building. People move, population patterns shift, and school districts are called upon to serve children and young adults who show up suddenly, unexpectedly. In a small school district, an additional forty or fifty unexpected students can be accommodated. In a large school district, where one housing development might bring thousands of additional students, and where construction of a new school takes years, the problems are momentous. Leased space is inherently flexible; the district rents space as it requires it, and moves out when the need lessens. There is no delay. Parents who plead for new schools because their schools are severely overcrowded often say, "My kids can't wait," as if a shovel put into the ground at that moment would help their children immediately. In a city like New York, six to eight years may pass from the time the building of a new school is proposed to the day it opens. It takes only months or even weeks to lease space and refurbish it.

Also, leasing of existing space does not tear apart neighborhoods, as school construction may do. In cities like New York, Philadelphia and Newark, building a school raises a host of problems: a site must be cleared, which usually means that some families lose their homes. Housing is perpetually in short supply, and further shrinks to the extent that schools replace dwellings. Yet we do it all the time.

It is often a senseless and cruel comedy. We make families homeless and force shopkeepers to relocate, so that children may have a school; what society gains on the one hand it loses on the other. There are children who need space today, so we undertake a building project that takes years to complete, and we tell the parents that their problem is being solved. The economics of construction dictate the building of *big* schools, and we inflict these on the young, though we know better. Because a new school building lasts fifty years or more, we commit educational programs more than a generation into the future to a style of education that is already obsolete. That future generations will need a capability for organized learning is a fair assumption, but to assume that the enterprise will require classrooms and auditoriums of the same kind that we have today and in the same geographical locations is absurd in this time of rapid, accelerating change. Yet few if any school districts have declared a moratorium on school construction. Indeed, most pursue it as if they had no choice.

A zero-construction building plan would reverse the priorities that tend to be reflected in school space decisions. Construction would be the last resort. The ten-month school year, now accepted as immutable, would be sharply questioned as a critical factor in the determination of school space need. Where it is now accepted that all high-school students belong in classrooms, the question would be asked, Must they *all* be in school *all* the time? Would not a high-school building accommodate more students if some of the students accomplished parts of their learning programs in jobs, or in public libraries, or doing independent study? Where there is now a tendency to ignore such things as industrial buildings and office buildings as potential school space, there would be a systematic district-wide inventory of potential school space, with records kept as to location, likely cost and adaptability for education programs. As the school district's population rose, the school board would not rush to the voters with a bond-issue question; the policy of zero construction would require that before a bond issue for new construction even was proposed, the public would have to be shown to its satisfaction that new construction was the only solution to the problem involved. A check list might look like this:

1. Is every existing school building fully in use? Or are some schools used at, say, 80 percent capacity, while others in the district are overcrowded? If so, why?

2. Are all large spaces in existing schools, including auditoriums, cafeterias, multipurpose rooms, foyers, lobbies and corridors, used at peak efficiency? Has an outside school-space expert, with the kind of vision displayed by E.F.L., been through the district to assess its use of school facilities? If not, why not?

3. Are there in the district "old" school buildings that are empty but still structurally sound? What consideration has been given to refurbishing such a building or buildings? Is restoration a possibility?

4. Would the need for space be better met by renovation of an existing school? (E.F.L. tells the story of a school district that needed at least one hundred additional elementary-school places. It could have built a conventional six-room wing on an existing school, and thereby obtained 150 seats at a cost of $240,000; instead, for an additional $7,000 it got 300 new seats—and a dramatically enhanced educational program for the entire school—by renovating the existing school structure, opening up space, removing walls, and making some additions.)

5. Would educational reorganization of one or more schools yield "new" space? Are the schools on a year-round calendar? Are they in maximum use each day? On what basis does the district justify the building of new schools if it uses the schools it has only nine or ten months a year, only six or seven hours a day?

6. Could high-school space be "expanded" by freeing more high-school students from the school building for parts of their educational programs? (To the extent that high-school students participate in work-study, apprenticeships, internships, independent study, and similar learning programs that take place outside the school, the school building is capable of serving more students—and learning becomes more real.) Would a significant number of high-school students want to attend school in the evening hours—a full-fledged evening high school starting in the late afternoon, serving dinner, and continuing into the evening? Has a survey asking this question been made by the district? If not, why not?

7. Has the district made an inventory of nonschool space within the boundaries of the school district? Has it inventoried potential space in office buildings and industrial buildings, in churches and museums, in public buildings, in vacant houses, and in housing developments? Has it exhausted the list? Is there absolutely no space in the district that is suitable and available on a rental, lease or purchase basis?

Ironically, the major consideration that has moved school boards and school administrators to look for alternatives to school construction has been the public's tendency in recent years to reject bond issues for such projects. In one year in the nineteen seventies, 53 out of every 100 bond-issue questions put to the voters were turned down. E.F.L. has concluded:

It is not an easy task these days to provide adequate school space of any kind. The rapid inflation of construction costs; the general slowdown in the nation's economy with its resulting unemployment; the sharp rise in educational costs—all these contribute to the reluctance of taxpayers to raise local property taxes. Whatever the specific causes may be, it is more difficult to pass a bond issue now than at any time since World War II. . . . Out of desperate necessity has come a burst of new thinking about the traditional American schoolhouse.

If desperate necessity is the mother of willingness to look at found space with official approbation, a keen sense of the future form of education is required to put such space to use with inventiveness and imagination. This is the hidden agenda of the zero-construction building plan: to use found space, in its diverse shapes and assorted sizes, as a tool to change the conventional ways in which schools are organized and operated. Can a high school of one hundred students housed in leased office space in the city's business district have the same rules and the same atmosphere as a conventional high school of three thousand students? Can an elementary school of eighty youngsters located in a public library be quite the same in content and style as the "regular" elementary school across the street?

The head of the school-planning effort in New York City is an intensely bright man named August Gold. He has spent a lifetime in that city's schools; he also has spent time working with E.F.L. Here he describes how space can be used to reform a school:

Facilities can serve as implements for the development of new patterns of instruction. Winston Churchill has frequently been quoted as saying, "First we shape our buildings, and then our buildings shape us." We might take this aphorism a step further, and plan facilities in such a way that they will determine the nature of the programs which they are to house. . . .

A number of projects undertaken in the New York City schools illumine this thesis. For instance, when a catering hall in the Bronx was rented for relief of overcrowding in a neighboring primary school, its large carpeted ballrooms suggested the possibility of "open classrooms," and led directly to the informalization of all teaching in that building. The open-education idea, sparked by the serendipity of the ballrooms, spread to the rest of the district in which wholesale transformation into "open space" and "open teaching" was soon under way.

Another district needed quarters for a bilingual school, and needed them in a hurry, to take advantage of available federal and state funds. For speed and economy, a small factory was converted into a series of large open carpeted spaces, each shared by five teachers. The obvious result was the development of team-teaching techniques to share talent as well as space, and a sharp turn toward flexibility and informalization.

So also with the instructional materials centers into which libraries have evolved. It is well-nigh impossible to conduct a classic "library lesson" on a whole-class basis in a space replete with carrels, small seminar rooms, cassette-style audio-visual equipment, and carpeted nooks and steps crying out for informality.

Individual independent thought and study is stimulated also by the arrangement and style of furniture. Fixed rows of seats guarantee uniformity, a condition difficult to maintain when the room is filled with trapezoidal tables, plastic cubes, snake-sofas, and bean-bag chairs. When socialized types of furniture are substituted for conventional desks and chairs, the result is invariably a simultaneous heightening of the group entente and a sharpening of distinctive personal characteristics.

The interior furnishings are also important if one wishes to stimulate imaginative play and artistic fancy. Left to their own devices, children create ingenious zones of privacy: packing-case shelters, under-table caves, scrap-wood and blanket partitions. Prescient designers have encouraged such creativity and imagination by introducing pipe-scaffolding, mezzanines, and sliding curtains, asymmetrical spacing, and even piles of assorted lumber and stacks of crates. Privacy, fantasy, art, and thoughtfulness go hand in hand and do not flourish in ranks and files.

Underlying all curriculum and all methodology is the need to develop a person's acceptance of the educative process. The client must be open to what is being offered; he cannot be successfully compelled to learn. Here too, facilities play a part—a warm and comfortable ambiance, signalled by shape, texture, color, light, temperature, sound, and the like, is basic. The soft carpet on the floor invites a sprawl with a book. Bright colors on the walls, drapes luxuriating at the windows, and pleasant grains in cabinet surfaces deliver a message of hospitality and friendliness which open the doors of the mind. Low levels and careful diffusion of light induce quiet and contemplation. Climate controlled against excessive heat and cold nourishes the senses; the air-conditioner, like the radiator, foments learning. If the objective is enrichment, the physical atmosphere must be rich.

Realistically, we do not expect school construction to cease. For one thing, some new schools have to be built, because there are places and situations where construction is the best alternative. For another, most of the public still believes that school construction is as inevitable as taxes, and as routinely necessary as brushing one's teeth. But shouldn't "zero construction" nonetheless be the goal of parents who understand the full meaning of the term and grasp its implications for school reform? For as long as school buildings continue to rise in monotonous similarity, the intellectual substance of the schools will tend to be as set as the mortar and bricks. The concrete features of the building will serve to determine, justify, explain and perpetuate the unchanging form of education offered inside. Today a school is built; a generation hence, some "radical" parents will propose a reform, and the response will come forth: Yes, but our school isn't made for that, and look what it would cost to make your idea fit—and the bonds aren't even paid off yet.

The practicality of this plan, and the foolishness of the practice of building schools as the first resort, is demonstrated by this account, published in January 1974 in the Springfield (Massachusetts) *Union:*

Becket—Two Berkshire County regional school systems are voicing concern over something other than the energy crisis—the increasing conversion rate of so-called leisure or seasonal homes into year-round residences.

Becket and Otis easily have been the Berkshire communities hardest hit by leisure home development in the past ten years. More recently, a growing number of these cottages and second homes are being occupied on a twelve-month basis by families with children. . . .

A conversion rate of only 10 to 15 percent could have a major impact on school enrollment, officials agree. . . .

The Central Berkshire School District has asked the voters in its seven member towns to approve multi-million [dollar] building programs several times in the last five years, and each time the plan has been defeated. . . .

Why doesn't the school district solve its problem by renting or purchasing one or more of the leisure homes in the district, and use them as schools? The capacity of the school system could be enlarged as quickly as a home could be leased or purchased; and when the trend reverses, which it may, the district will not have millions of dollars of school buildings on its hands standing empty or nearly empty. Whatever the motivations of the voters who have been rejecting bond-issue proposals, they have shown more common sense than the planners.

PLAN VII / *The High-School-Renewal Plan*

The following description of a high school is from a report commissioned by an urban school system in the Northeast:

The needs of the student body at _____ High School are as varied as the student body itself. The most obvious problem is the tension between American black students and Dominican students. . . . There are several streetgang-type organizations among the Dominicans. . . . According to students involved in these organizations, they developed as social clubs and started to be used for self-defense as tensions developed in the community and the school. . . .

There are several pressing educational problems involving large numbers of Dominican students. Many do not speak English, and many more speak some English but cannot read or write English on a high-school level. Some have had little or no formal education in the Dominican Republic. To most, there is [a] feeling of not belonging, of being in an alien environment. . . . Dominican students resent being referred to as "Spanish-speaking." They don't want to be lumped together with Puerto Rican and other Latin groups. They feel that the staff cannot distinguish them from other Latin groups, and this is resented. They feel that most Spanish-oriented programs and clubs . . . are geared to Puerto Ricans. Many feel that there is nothing for them. . . .

The black students . . . are fearful of the Dominicans, especially since the Dominicans outnumber them in any confrontation. . . .

The white students are the most fearful. They do not go to the cafeteria. They eat in class or during office jobs. . . . White students leave the school area immediately upon dismissal. . . .

One problem which envelops the school is its past history of disrup-

66

tion and violence. Staff morale is very low. Most teachers are fearful, and some have become suspicious of all the students. . . . The students who are feared deeply resent their being feared to that extent by adults. . . . The teachers are reluctant to participate in any type of security program. Contributing to this reluctance is a feeling that they will get little or no backing from the administration. They also feel that the courts return to the school those who, in their eyes, have committed outrageous acts. . . .

The supervisory staff was office-bound. Some were unaware of uncovered classes within their own departments. When there were disturbances nearby, they remained in their offices. For the most part, they seem to be remote from the students.

There seem also to be problems of communication and understanding between the principal and the staff. The staff feels that the principal does not consult with them, or inform them about the things he is doing or plans to do. On the other hand, the principal feels that the staff is not cooperative. He feels that he does not have their support. As a result, there [have been] bad feelings and recriminations. . . .

Membership [in the parent organization] has been very low. There have been no meetings. . . . All efforts to involve Dominican parents [in a reorganization effort] have failed. . . .

More bilingual teachers are needed. . . .

There is a lack of attractive offerings by the English, Social Studies, Science and Industrial Arts departments. For example, there are no courses dealing with the history, culture or literature of Latin America.

The cafeteria is a focal point where disturbances are generated and festered. Many students spend several periods in the cafeteria. Some attend few if any classes. Rumors of alleged inequities flow freely. . . . Groups continue to be polarized, and rivalries are evident. . . .

There is a need for more black and Hispanic paraprofessionals, teachers and supervisors. . . . A program is also needed to allay fears and reduce tensions among the students. . . . There are in the school at least a dozen ethnic groups with strong national ties and cultural identities. . . There is a need for community and parent participation. . . .

This description, several years old, is not, unfortunately, entirely out of date. It is not that the principal has not tried, or that the city has chosen to ignore the school; it is that the ills have deep roots. It is simpler to describe the problems of high schools than to prescribe treatment. The obstacles are high, far higher than any outsider might suspect. While high-school principals are not our favorite species of educational leader, because too few of them provide genuine leadership, one must concede this point: to run a high school, and to do it well, is one of the most trying jobs in public education these days. Because this is so, and because their training typically is so woefully irrelevant, and because high schools tend to be tragically dysfunctional mostly as the result of a distorted perception of their role, this portrait of a high-school hell-hole is not a blight on an otherwise harmonious landscape. It reflects hundreds of high schools in dozens of cities. Even suburbia's high schools, where the most impressive statistics of family background are found, and where student achievement and numbers of graduates who proceed to college are high, are in deep trouble. The suburban high school may be less incident-prone than its big-city counterpart; its students may be less inclined to form street gangs to achieve social identity and group protection; but, in substantial numbers, they find their high schools alien, hostile, and deaf to their need for drastic educational and organizational change—much as do their city colleagues. If angry frustration characterizes the state of mind of many high-school students in the cities, spiritual depression describes the attitude of many high-school students in the suburbs. Hopelessness has more than one root and manifests itself in different ways.

We do not propose to have ready-made solutions or patent medicines for troubled high schools with wide arrays of problems. Still, there may be a common process for finding ways to make schools more habitable and, finally, more functional. Whether it will work, we do not know, for it has not been tried on anything like the scale we propose.

The High-School-Renewal Plan would work like this:

1. A high school would end its regular courses on a prearranged date, with the informed consent of staff, students and parents, and, instead of the usual courses and programs, would involve all the students and staff, as well as interested parents, in a project to replan the school—or, really, to plan a "new" one.

However it may be organized, whatever its ground rules, the process would involve each student and each staff member, and would fill the entire school day. For the duration of the project, the planning process *is* the educational program: for the student, it replaces a schedule of courses; for the teacher, it takes the place of the lesson plan and the syllabus.

2. Everybody who participates would work as a school planner, with one man/one vote the guiding principle, and work out the rules and organization.

3. The principal, who is chief planner, would be responsible for making sure that the planners have what they need—meeting rooms, secretarial services, and so forth—and that they move forward on their agenda. But by no means would the principal have veto power; he has a vote, and the right to participate in the work.

4. As chief planner, the principal would set a deadline, as a rule of thumb no shorter than three months and no longer than a school year. There should be enough time for serious and thorough planning; but there should also be a sense of urgency and immediacy.

5. To get more out of the whole exercise, and to solicit sound recommendations, outside authorities would be enlisted from such fields as sociology, anthropology, psychology, law, politics, political science, management, the behavioral sciences, organizational theory, et cetera. These advisers may come from nearby universities and colleges, government agencies, or private industry. They are not to be visiting lecturers, but co-workers in organizing the methodology, setting clear agendas, and reaching consensus on findings and recommendations.

6. The combined findings are then issued:

First, a concrete statement concerning the meaning of high-school education and the work of a high school. The planners must answer two fundamental questions: What constitutes the education of a high-school graduate in contemporary American society? What role does, or should, the high school play in affording individuals the opportunity to earn a diploma?

Second, a list of the specific learning needs of the school's students, and of the needed educational resources (school and nonschool).

Third, job descriptions and definitions of the roles to be played by staff and students.

Fourth, specific recommendations, in keeping with the findings, as to how to reorganize and govern the school as a defined community of citizens, each of whom has rights and responsibilities toward himself and his fellow citizens.

What happens to the "education" of the students during the planning process—the programs in English and history, math, civics and science? Student-planners would receive the same number of school credits they would have received had they been enrolled in the old standard program, credits being applied as best the staff can figure to subject areas. Unconventional perhaps, but student-planners should get credit for this work just as teacher-planners are paid their regular salaries. If the plan is worth undertaking, it is worth paying for, in dollars and in credits.

What of the recommendations? As far as practicable, they should be put to work, the school being reorganized to the maximum extent, and with maximum efficiency (which means speed). The planning idea needs the strong and explicit support, therefore, of the school principal, as well as of the school district administrators and the district board. The understanding should be that the planners' design will become reality, so long as it does not contravene the law. The recommendations are to be transformed by the principal and higher authority into regulation and policy.

What if the planners make recommendations that the principal views as unreasonable? How is a stand-off to be resolved? The answer must be, democratically. The planners must have the right to appeal up to the next level of authority, and ultimately to the school board. They may lose, but at least that is the way the democratic political process works. Would not students learn a lot, even if they lose some points on appeal? The risk of disillusion is worth the real chance that students—very likely for the first time—will feel the weight and pride of responsibility, and experience the dynamics of real politics waged for real stakes.

How does a school begin this enormously complex project? Given the different traditions and differing pressures of various high schools, we are not sure. It seems likely that different schools may have different approaches, as well as different planning procedures. But we would make these general points: Whoever brings the issue into the open—whoever suggests that the plan be tried—the support, or at least the tolerance, of the principal and his school district supervisors up to and including the school board must be achieved in advance so as to protect the integrity of the planning process and to guarantee that its recommendations will be implemented. Parents too must be won over to the notion that the undertaking is not an effort by a group of students and sympathetic teachers to shirk their responsibilities to learn and to teach, but is a real effort by students and teachers to take on a higher level of responsibility, that they want to improve their school, make it more useful to more students, make it less tense (and safer), and make it a working example of American democracy (and a model of citizenship). The initial advocates might be well advised to consider a preplanning session, where they would get together for a week or two, to formulate specifics. The first question of skeptical school authorities and parents will be: How will it work? The preplanning session should have developed specific answers to this very fair question.

Is the project important enough educationally to call a moratorium on conventional course work over an extended period? The answer is that its educational value will pretty much reflect the importance that the school authorities place on it, and the support that they give it. If school authorities make it clear to staff, students and parents that they regard the planning as a serious undertaking, that they will implement the recommendations, the educational value of the experience will be high.

The plan would cost very little. School would be open the same number of hours each day, and the same number of days each week. No additional staff and no special equipment or materials are required. The only extra requirement is the outside consultants. A small fund likely would be necessary to cover the costs of travel, expenses and fees for such help. Perhaps the principal would be able to raise this money locally, from private industry or business or community organizations, or from a foundation. If not, the principal might convert one or two staff positions into dollars, and use that to cover the extra costs. In a high school of two thousand students or more, several staff positions become vacant almost every year as people retire or move to other jobs; since planning would temporarily replace classroom teaching, leaving one or two vacancies unfilled would be logical and would provide the necessary funds.

Obviously, the project could not and should not be attempted in the face of substantial opposition from students or parents. Where the opposition is relatively slight, however, the plan can be initiated, as long as those who don't wish to participate are given the option of going to another school. Timing, needless to say, is important; if those who do choose to go to another school have sufficient time to make their plans, they will be far less likely to complain.

While the support of teachers is highly desirable and should be sought, it can be expected that some teachers in a large high school will not approve of the idea. In any case, the opposition of some teachers should not stop the plan where a majority of parents and students, as well as the principal and some of the teachers, want to try it. The school belongs to the public, not to the employed staff. The rights of a teacher who disapproves of the plan should be protected, in that he or she should not be forced to participate in it, but should be offered the chance to transfer to another school in the district and to a comparable teaching job. Timing again is critical—last-minute, hastily made transfers are distasteful. They are also unnecessary when a plan is initiated openly, systematically, diplomatically, and with a common-sense rationale that says, "The purpose is not to disrupt the lives of teachers or anyone else, but to improve a school with a long history of severe trouble."

Doesn't this plan ask an awful lot of a school? It does indeed—nothing less than the total, complete shutdown of an entire high-school program for an extended period of time in the hope—and it is merely a hope—that the time can be better spent to find a new and better way of conducting school business. There is no guarantee that the process will be free of conflict; there is every likelihood that it will be a tense experience and that tempers will fly on more than a few occasions. There is the possibility that students, because of their numbers, will dominate and that their maturity will not be all that we adults would like it to be. There is the chance that the staff will on occasion resort to pulling rank to control the planning and protect their special interests. There is the likelihood that very few parents will participate over the long haul, and that those who do may not be representative of the larger community. Yet, if a school is deeply troubled, what will be lost? Isn't it better to attempt something radically different rather than keep on conducting school business mindlessly, fearfully, painfully, with failure increasing each day? If personal and professional relations are so doubtful and fraught with danger and frustrations—as they are in the school described —how much "education" can really be lost if regular subject-matter is not covered for a semester or a year? If a school is peaceful for a time simply because of the novelty of not going to classes in the old routine, that might be an achievement in itself.

The planners, one hopes, would deal with every aspect of their school. Perhaps they will sketch out the beginnings of a new system of internal government, with student and faculty congresses to legislate rules, school courts to hear charges and set penalties; with a written constitution of student, staff and parent rights, and with procedures for guaranteeing due process to each member of the school community. Maybe they will rewrite the school's diploma standards, or set basic requirements for alternative (non-school) learning programs, or draft procedures for establishing a system in which every student in his tenth and eleventh years has a twelfth-year student as his student adviser and personal tutor. Perhaps they will conceive a compelling rationale for expanded work opportunities for students for which the school would give credits for experience thus gained; or for students to spend more time in community service work; or for the school to take more advantage of community resources as educational resources increasingly open to students who wish to learn in non-school settings part time or full time.

But whatever the matters on which the planners spend most of their time, the value to students is obvious: youth of high-school age, on the threshold of full voting citizenship, need the opportunity—perhaps more than anything else—to learn how to make their way in life by working cooperatively with other people whose backgrounds, goals and ways of thinking may be quite different from their own. They need the experience of responsibility; and they need to learn the intricacies, the potential and the pain of functioning in a democratic setting. They need the opportunity to ask questions; and they need to be challenged to devise workable solutions to educational and social problems that perplex us all, including their teachers and their parents. They deserve the chance to learn at first hand that running a school is hard work, and that making it work to the satisfaction of all concerned is still more difficult. These are lessons nobody can get from a book or a lecture, only from personal experience. What more valuable service could a high school provide than to turn out graduates who are experienced in governing their lives?

What, after all, is an alternative for the troubled high school? What noble mission is served by holding involuntary students for five or six hours a day—on the days on which they bother to come to school at all? What lessons in democratic living are being taught by the high school that tests the citizenship of its students by how well they conform to rules and regulations written in the privacy of the principal's office and executed in a manner which the students perceive as arbitrary and authoritarian? How much responsibility is cultivated and nurtured in the individual by a high school which gives the individual no chances to experience responsibility?

One alternative for the troubled high school is more security guards, more police. Unless the school makes it possible for its students to state what they want and to show what they themselves can do; unless it affords them some worthwhile opportunities to govern their own lives and be responsible for the consequences of their own decisions; until the school accepts the fact that one of the causes of antisocial behavior on the part of students is the nature of the school itself, those in command of the school are likely to find it more and more necessary to watch students as they move around from class to meaningless class. They will have to resign themselves to careers that have more to do with penology than with education.

Perhaps the most basic obstacle to bringing parents closer to the decision-making process in schools is the sheer size of school districts. By the end of the 1960s, the public schools of the United States enrolled, in round figures, 45.5 million students. Four fifths of them (again using round figures) were in school districts that enrolled more than 2,500 students. More than half of this four-fifths group—that is, more than 40 percent of the nation's students—were in districts with enrollments of 10,000 or more. Because the trend is, and has been, toward greater consolidation of school districts, it is reasonable to assume that even more children, proportionally, are in school districts that enroll more than 2,500 students today.

School districts of this magnitude do have advantages, of course. There often is economy in size. Also, there is the greater likelihood that a relatively large school district, because of its comparatively large population and tax base, will have more sophisticated educational programs and facilities than would a smaller, more isolated district.

But size also tends to place distance between school decisions and parents. Once a district has several thousand students and an annual budget in the millions of dollars, the inherent largeness and complexity of day-to-day decisions make it less and less likely that parents will participate directly. Professionals and experts take over, and because the problems appear so complicated and technical, most parents are quite willing to let them. The inevitable result is that most parents—in spite of school rhetoric about the value of "local" control over education—do not exercise much influence over their own schools, about how the budget is spent, how programs are designed and operated, how the staff is evaluated, how and what children are taught, who is hired and who gets tenure, who the principal is, what the rules and regulations are that govern schools.

In the nation's largest cities—New York and Detroit are the best examples—the distance between parents and schools was a basic reason for recent moves to "decentralize" the schools. Carving a massive school system—New York has more than 1.1 million students, more than 900 schools, a total faculty that could be seated together only in a major-league baseball stadium—would thrust parents closer to their schools; this, at least, was the idea. Even with decentralization, however, it's difficult for the parents to get close to their child's school and into its decision-making process. To cite New York again, decentralization of that city's massive school system has created thirty-two community school districts, each with its own elected board of education and its own superintendent of schools. Because New York City is so large, however, these "community" districts are themselves overwhelming in size—most of them have 25,000 students each, or close to it; some have more. Each of these thirty-two districts, in other words, approximates the size of the school district of Syracuse, New York, a reasonably large city by most standards.*

This is not to suggest that the historical trend of school-district consolidation should be reversed and the districts should be par-

* In essence, it is our belief that when the New York State legislature decentralized the schools of New York City it did not go nearly far enough. If it truly wished to decentralize the schools, it should have carved the system into 100 or more community districts and vested far more power in the community districts than it has thus far. The schools of New York City remain under central influence in many critical areas, including the hiring of teachers. In this respect, the word "decentralization" is a misleading term; it leads people to think much more has been done than really has been. Nor would this kind of thorough decentralization exacerbate racial isolation in schools necessarily; decentralized districts in a city are subject to the same laws as other districts in New York State. Moreover, the record of big-city, centralized school systems with regard to promoting integrated learning is hardly laudable, especially in the North, where school decentralization is more of an issue because the cities are larger.

titioned into smaller, separate school systems. This would be not only impractical, but also highly questionable. But there ought to be a way (or ways) of moving parents much closer to the decisions that schools make about children. Not only would school-parent relations be improved, but, more important, parents would begin to assert new control over schools and assume a new level of responsibility for the formal education of their children. These developments, it seems to us, are critical both to the serious reform of schools and to the emphasis on the primary role and responsibility of parents in the education of their own children.*

We believe that parents should be directly involved in the most fundamental decisions that schools make: the selection of a principal, the hiring of teachers and other staff, tenure decisions, the formulation of a budget (since a budget is a dollars-and-cents expression of programs for children), the evaluation of staff, the setting of rules and regulations that govern daily operation of the school, the planning of new educational programs. To this end, and in keeping with the belief that direct parent involvement in schools is a powerful tool for school reform, we propose what we call the Autonomous-School Plan.

The plan is basically this:

A school district would designate a school an "autonomous school" for a trial period of one year or more.† Since the central

---

* Parent education, in fact, is more important than the education of children, in the sense that the attitudes toward life and the level of discourse in a home are crucial factors in what a child learns and the value he or she places on learning. Thus, to the extent that parents become more educated and sophisticated about schools through their involvement in school decisions, the intellectual atmosphere of the home is enhanced, and positive attitudes toward learning are fostered in children in more powerful ways than most schools ever could hope to accomplish. This aspect of parent involvement in school decision-making has yet to receive the attention it warrants. This reasoning accounts, in part, for the extraordinary amount of time Harvey Scribner spent in meetings with parents, and efforts his administration made to involve parents in decision-making, while he was Chancellor of the New York City schools. Interestingly, this commitment of time to parent groups often was criticized by school professionals, who complained they were not getting enough time with the head of the school system.

† For simplicity of explanation we have described this idea in the context of a single school. This should not be taken to mean that we recommend every school district have just one "autonomous school." All schools in a

purpose of the plan would be to turn over effective control of the school to the parents involved, the desire of parents for the plan obviously is essential. The district, therefore, would not act until and unless it had the clear approval of a large majority of parents in a given school—about two thirds would seem to be a good rule of thumb.

Long before the plan is to be implemented, district school officials and parents would draft a clear, written description of how the plan would work, including detailed operating procedures. The plan would set forth a governance system and would spell out the roles and responsibilities of parents, principal, district school board and district superintendent. The plan could take the form of a policy statement or contract, or a combination of the two. Besides parents, the principal and superintendent should be closely involved in the formulation of the plan to insure their future support of it. The pivotal element of the plan would be governance of the school by an elected body of parents.

The draft plan would be sent to the district school board for preliminary approval. After this approval, the plan would be circulated to all families with children in the proposed "autonomous school," and thorough discussion of the plan would follow. Ultimately, each family would be asked to decide whether it wishes to participate—by having children in the school.

If the parents of approximately two thirds of the children say they want to try the plan, the district would move ahead to implement it. A starting date would be set—most likely the beginning of the next school year. The families who choose not to participate would be given optional assignments for their children at nearby schools,* and student places which thus become avail-

---

district should be made autonomous as quickly as the district can establish them as such. Ideally, every school would be autonomous, run by elected parents under the aegis of a district board of education.

* We recognize the possibility of increased isolation of racial and economic minorities that conceivably could result from the selective shifting of children from school to school as this plan spread across a school district. This possibility, however, is neither inevitable nor tolerable. In no way would we release a school district from its legal, moral and educational responsibility to provide for integrated learning.

able would be offered to other parents who are attracted by the plan. This volunteer aspect of the plan is most important. Any new venture in education will have enough problems without having to contend with unwilling participants. Moreover, a venture of this kind clearly should not be forced on parents who don't want it; those who prefer conventional forms of school should have the right to choose them.

Before the plan is to take effect, the participating families would elect a governing body. Each family with one or more children in school would get one vote, based on the principle of one family/one vote. The district should work hard and with care to ensure that the election is well publicized, that all voting families have pertinent information concerning the parents running for seats on the governing board, and that all (or nearly all) families cast their vote. By the time of the election, the district school board would give final approval to the operating plan.

The elected governing board of parents would operate the school in keeping with the plan adopted by the district school board. It would set policy for its school much as the district board sets policy for the district as a whole.

The governing board would receive from the district a lump-sum budget to operate the school for a year, the total representing the school's fair share of local, state and federal dollars, plus any special moneys, such as from private sources or foundation grants, which might be due the school. The governing board would ask its principal to draw up a budget within the total allowance, which ultimately would be approved by the board. The principal would be held to the approved budget; he would not be allowed to deviate from it without the express approval of the governing board any more than the district school superintendent could alter the district budget without the approval of the district school board.

The governing board would have the right and responsibility to evaluate all the school's educational programs and projects, replace those it feels ought to be replaced, expand those it believes are worthy of expansion, and institute new programs as long as it has sufficient funds in its budget.

The board would employ new teachers and other staff as positions become vacant. If the principal leaves, the board would select a successor. As should be obvious, in filling such positions the board would be required to comply with district policies, such as equal employment opportunities, teacher transfer rights, and teacher contracts that apply district-wide. The choice of person, however, would be the board's.

The board would meet as often as necessary in public meeting to act on recommendations brought to it by its chief administrator, the principal. As a means of keeping parents informed, it would issue reports and newsletters. In addition, it would hold meetings periodically at which any parent or staff member would be allowed to address the board for several minutes on any school topic.*

The board would set the rules and regulations for the school, and hold the principal accountable for administering them. It would evaluate teachers and administrators, or have the principal do it for the board.

Most important of all, perhaps, the governing board would work with parents and staff to define a set of simple goals, and near the end of the year the board would measure the school's performance against these goals. This self-evaluation report (which need not be elaborate), together with the stated goals and a breakdown of the school's budget, would constitute the governing board's official accounting to the school district on how the school's allocated funds were spent and what was accomplished.

The reform potential of written goals should not be overlooked. Goals are basic to a sense of purpose and function. What is a school for? How should it touch the lives of children? How should it serve parents and families? How does it relate to the home? What can it do for children, and what *should* it do? How can it harm children, and therefore what should it avoid doing?

---

* Much to its credit, the central Board of Education in New York City does this monthly. It's an amazingly informative meeting, and a very useful means for board members and administrators to hear about problems they never knew existed.

As long as we have schools, what does every child deserve from his?

A range of rudimentary goals can tell you what the authors of the goals envision a school to be, what they perceive as its mission, what they believe ought to be the criteria for evaluating a school's successes and failings. The simplest goals often are the most insightful and revealing. "The emphasis must be upon learning, rather than teaching." This is the first goal in a document known as the Vermont Design for Education.* "Education is a process conceived to benefit the learner," the Vermont Design continues. "Central to any focus is the individual and how his learning process may be maximized. This idea is basic and provides the foundation for all other elements of quality education."

The statement, set forth as a goal, is simple yet almost profound; it makes clear by implication how a school's success or failure may be measured. Whatever the style of the school—open classroom, traditional, bilingual, Montessori—the evaluative criterion is the same: Is the emphasis on teaching or learning? Is the process beneficial to the learner? Is the individual learner central?

The rest of the goals in the Vermont Design are equally simple:

A student must be accepted as a person. . . .

Education should be based upon the individual's strong, inherent desire to learn and to make sense of his environment. . . .

All people need success to prosper. Youth is no exception. . . .

Education should strive to maintain the individuality and originality of the learner. The school's function is to expand the differences between individuals and create a respect for those differences.

---

* The Vermont Design for Education was published in 1969 by the Vermont Department of Education when Harvey Scribner was its Commissioner. The department did not mandate its goals on local school systems, but did require each school district to devise its own goals or "design." The process of formulating goals was undertaken by virtually all school districts in Vermont over the span of several years, including long after Scribner left Vermont for New York City.

Emphasis should be upon a child's own way of learning—through discovery and exploration—through real rather than abstract experiences. . . .

The development of an individual's thought process should be primary. . . . The ability to solve problems, whether social, mathematical, or economic must be given preference. . . .

People should perceive the learning process as related to their own sense of reality. . . .

An individual must be allowed to work according to his own abilities. Students are as diverse intellectually as they are physically. . . . Learning experiences must be geared to individual needs rather than group norms.

The teacher's role must be that of a partner and guide in the learning process. . . . The teacher does not abdicate his leadership role in the student-centered approach, but indeed assumes a far more important role of leadership, one responding to the individualized needs of each person with whom he works.

The development of a personal philosophy, a basic set of values, is perhaps one of the most important of human achievements. The school must assume an active role in helping each individual to evolve a set of personal values. . . .

We must seek to individualize our expectations of a person's progress as we strive to individualize the learning experiences for each person. . . . We must develop personalized ways of assessing an individual's progress. . . .

The environment within which students are encouraged to learn must be greatly expanded. The classroom, or even the school, is an extremely limited learning environment. The total culture surrounding each individual should become his learning environment. . . . The wealth of personal talent in the community should be utilized. . . .

The school should provide a structure in which students can learn from each other. . . .

To provide a maximum learning experience for all students requires the involvement and support of the entire community. . . .

Schools should be compatible with reality. Learning which is compartmentalized into artificial subject fields by teachers and administrators is contrary to what is known about the learning process. . . .

Individuals should be encouraged to develop a sense of responsibility. . .

These obviously are not the only goals that a governing board in an autonomous school could agree on. But they are incisive examples of how simple statements of purpose can be potentially revolutionary.

If a governing board had this set of goals to work with, it could ask its principal and itself: How does this school measure up? Is every child accepted for what he or she is? Or do we label some children "fast learners," "slow learners," "troubled," "hyperactive," "unorganized," "can't follow instructions," "disruptive," "handicapped," "disadvantaged," "lazy," "unmotivated"? Does every child get the chance to succeed at something each day, however minor the "something" may seem? Or do some children face chronic failure every hour, every day? Do we emphasize creativity, originality and the development of problem-solving abilities? Or do we emphasize rote learning—the teach-'em-and-test-'em approach? Does this school make use of nonschool people and places? How much use? The answers to such questions may not fill shelves like the spiral-bound evaluation reports that come out of professional consulting firms, but they may be more helpful, far less expensive, and more likely to generate change.

The idea of autonomous schools is hardly radical. It does not call for abolishing school boards—they would still be needed to set district policies, much as state departments of education set state policies that affect local school districts and negotiate contracts with organized teachers and other staff unions, and monitor the parent governing boards to make sure they comply with federal and state laws, district policies, and their own rules of procedure. The plan does not envision parents replacing teachers in the classroom, or firing them wholesale, or discriminating against some teachers or favoring others. (This is not a plan to place parents above the law.) Extra costs are not involved. If anything, parents would be affected most seriously; they would be required to assume a new level of direct responsibility for decision-making.

How radical is it to suggest that parents who send their children to school should democratically elect some representatives to run those schools? Is it radical to suggest that the best government usually is the government closest to the governed? If parents should be involved and concerned with schools—and schools continually complain of parent apathy—why not give parents something to come into school for? Are parents supposed to be heard from only when a bond issue to build a new school is to go before the voters, and to be seen only during American Education Week?

This idea would not raise any problem that is more complicated than negotiating a contract with teachers in a moderately sized city, or clearing a site for a new high school in downtown Chicago. To oppose it is, in reality, to say, "No, I don't believe parents are sophisticated or knowledgeable enough to administer a school"—in which case we ought to begin to limit seats on all school boards to professional educators. Or it is to say, "No, running schools isn't a job for parents—that's a job for professionals"—which is to reject the American political theory of public control of education, to raise professionals to a level of expertise the profession does not possess, and to absolve parents of direct responsibility for the education of children.

PLAN IX / *The External-Diploma Plan*

In public schooling, everything academic ultimately points toward the diploma. The high-school diploma is the symbol of the culmination of a person's formal schooling, the sign of completion of a sequence of studies lasting twelve or thirteen years, the imprimatur of the institution—its seal of approval—on a person's educational attainment in subject areas commonly accepted as important to enlightened, functioning citizenship. Because the diploma is the most important document the school issues to a student, the award of a diploma is a ceremonial occasion. Parents, teachers—themselves graduates of schools—gather to witness the handing of diplomas to their children and students. Graduation exercises are more than a familiar ritual; they are an American folkway.

Every high school in the land issues diplomas; and as glad as each of us is to receive one, few of us could place our hands on our diplomas if asked. We bury them in cartons, store them in attics and cellars, lose them, file them away, tuck them in bookcases; some of us hang them on a wall. We treat these documents with little respect, which is strange, considering the work we did to earn them and the psychological value we place on them.

Our thoughtlessness, however unconscious it may be, is nonetheless quite apt. Diplomas, as documents, are without value. There is no market for old high-school diplomas. More important, they have no absolute meaning, because there is no single standard that the holders of all diplomas meet. There never has been anything analogous to a gold standard for high-school diplomas; for all the talk about "standards," no two high-school diplomas in existence can be taken to mean that the two individuals who hold them are the same by any educational measure. In truth—though we don't think of it this way—the "standards" for a high-school diploma vary not only from school to school, even in the same city, but also from graduate to graduate of the same school. Who can say that the diplomas issued by George Washington High School today are issued for the same educational reasons as fifty years ago, or twenty or ten? Who can say, indeed, that any two graduates in the same graduating class at George Washington earned their diplomas by meeting precisely the same criteria? Did they have the same teachers, take the same courses, receive the same grades? Did they each study a foreign language? Over the twelve-year span of their school careers, did they go to school the same number of days? Did they attend the same elementary schools? Do they read at the same rate? Is one more talented in art, the other more skilled in biology? Is one more skilled with his hands, the other more able at negotiating and problem-solving? One diploma, one set of standards? No, the effective standards were as unique as the two individuals.

In point of specific accomplishment, the only things we know for sure about people who own a high-school diploma are that they went to school for about twelve years (possibly more if they went to kindergarten, possibly fewer if their education was accelerated); that they were satisfactorily processed through the required courses; and that they weren't expelled. As disappointing and negative as this may sound, that's all we know with certainty. This is not to depreciate the diploma, but to make the point that we should not fool ourselves about what a diploma is and what it signifies. It is a credential, a ticket that allows the holder to pass through certain gates—the gates to college, to employment, to civil-service examinations. Those who tend the gates know the diploma is not necessarily a guarantee of ability, skill or performance, but they cash the document for a chance at college, at a job, or the chance to take a test for government employment. The utility of the diploma is limited to this: the opportunities it makes available.

The "external-diploma plan" concerns diplomas to be earned by persons who aren't in school any more and may not have been in school for years, diplomas to be granted on the basis of demonstrated competence to perform, not time spent in school. It is a common-sense idea, but strong objections will be raised, and the first no doubt will have to do with "standards." "This," we can hear it said, "will lower standards." "Why can't 'they' earn diplomas the way we did?" "My children have been raised to go to school and work hard so they can get diplomas—it isn't fair to them to give diplomas to people who haven't done that." "What good are diplomas if everybody gets them?" "We're not doing 'them' a favor if we lower standards and give out worthless diplomas."

STANDARDS. The concept is built on sand, but few will admit it. The notion of standards may be a cultivated myth, a phantom piece of educational baggage, but this does not diminish the battle. Professionals are constantly telling the public about *standards*. The public likes to hear it said that their schools have *standards*, that the diplomas they earned as students were based on *standards*. It's nonsense, but it works; we like to be assured that education is based on something constant, eternal and universal, something concrete and valuable.

The diplomas that schools give out today are based on one noneducational standard: time spent in school. If you last twelve (or thirteen) years in the system, the diploma is yours; if you leave early, the diploma is denied—you're a dropout. No matter what you do in life, how successful you are, how knowledgeable you become, there is no second chance to obtain the high-school diploma—unless you return to school and put in the required time.

You *can* get something called an "equivalency" diploma. Most states offer this document to anyone who takes and passes a series of written tests on basic skills, such as reading, social studies and arithmetic. The military services administer similar batteries of tests to thousands of dropouts entering the Army, Navy and Air Force. From the two—state education departments and the

Pentagon—tens of thousands of Americans have equivalency diplomas, in place of regular diplomas from regular schools.

Interestingly, the equivalency diplomas are recognized and accepted by universities and colleges, employers in private industry and civil-service examiners. But not by high schools—the schools that in a very real sense failed the dropout in the first instance. In short, if you drop out of school and later earn an equivalency diploma from the state, the document will allow you to apply for admission to a university or college, obtain a job, or permit you to take civil-service examinations for government positions. But if you take the equivalency diploma to the high school you dropped out of, the principal will say, "Fine, now if you want our diploma, these are the courses you'll have to make up." In the school's view, the word *equivalency* does not mean *the equivalent of* the school's diploma, it means different from and less than. It matters not that the rest of the world recognizes the document; the standard of the school—time in the classroom—has not been met.

The external-diploma idea substitutes performance for time-in-school as the central criterion for granting diplomas—for those individuals who leave school without a diploma and choose later to earn one using this method. The plan would in no way stop schools from awarding diplomas as they always have done and continue to do. The plan simply would establish an additional path for people who want a second chance and are willing to have their performance in the real world judged. This would take away nothing from students in school, unless they or their parents (or their teachers and principals) feel that their diplomas are valuable only to the extent that large numbers of other people are denied diplomas.

An External-Diploma Plan might work like this:

A school district, under a policy adopted by its board of education in public meeting, would agree to grant its regular high-school diploma to any person living within its jurisdiction who lacks a diploma and fits one of these conditions:

1. The applicant has earned an equivalency diploma from the state or from one of the military services. Upon presentation of

the equivalency document, a district high school would issue in addition its own diploma.

2. The applicant has entered a recognized university, college or community college—there are individuals who do get into college without high-school diplomas—and has successfully completed one year's studies. On presentation of evidence to this effect (a transcript of the student's college record would do), the district would issue a diploma.

3. The applicant is working in a job generally considered to be at a level requiring high-school graduates—civil-service employees in post offices and government agencies, noncommissioned officers in the military services, salesmen, secretaries, office workers, bank tellers, business-machine operators, computer programmers, technicians, and so on. The school district would set guidelines spelling out the kinds of jobs that qualify. The diploma applicant would ask the district to have his or her on-the-job performance evaluated. The district in turn would ask the applicant's supervisor at the job to evaluate the applicant's work performance for a period of six months or a year. If the supervisor reports back that the applicant performed at least as well on the job as high-school graduates on the same or comparable jobs, the district would grant a diploma.

If a district is concerned that external diplomas might encourage some students to drop out of school as a way of fleeing the classroom and getting a diploma ahead of their classmates, the district would limit external diplomas to persons whose high-school class has graduated. (In fact, state equivalency diploma programs generally do this.)

If a district is concerned about "standards," we would submit that external diplomas are entirely justifiable and defensible, based as they would be on a person's demonstrated capacity to perform. If diplomas are supposed to signify that a person can perform at a certain level, does it make sense to deny diplomas to people who have earned equivalency diplomas from the state, have been admitted to college and done a year's work there, or have gotten a job at a high-school graduate's level and are performing as competently as high-school graduates?

Finally, if a district is concerned about costs, the cost of running an external-diploma project would not be prohibitive. It would require no school buildings, no teachers, no principals. It would require only a small administrative staff to process applications and issue diplomas, in keeping with policies and regulations established by school-district authorities. In unusual instances where the project staff could not determine whether a diploma should be issued, the case would be referred to the superintendent of schools or the board of education.

This plan would not replace or dislodge existing—and valuable —programs for dropouts, adults, out-of-school youth, and returning military veterans. Such programs, offering basic education courses and often preparing people to take equivalency-diploma tests, would continue to be needed. Though this plan would not displace such programs, it would lend incentive to the people in them. They would have evidence that their kind of learning, their program, can lead to the same document that regular high-school graduates receive. They might feel, for the first time, that they are part of a larger public-education enterprise, and that they are not second-class students working for a second-rate diploma. ("It may be equal but it's not the same," someone said disparagingly of the equivalency diploma at a public hearing in New York City during the time we were there.)

Nor would external diplomas replace equivalency diplomas;* there's nothing wrong with equivalency diplomas as long as they are recognized as equivalent to regular diplomas and are treated as such. If they are, common sense says they should be interchangeable.†

* The number of people taking equivalency tests as a way of getting a diploma likely would be cut down if substantial numbers of school districts adopted external-diploma plans. The result would be a savings to the states in administering equivalency tests and preparing people to take them.
† In New York City, state equivalency diplomas can be exchanged for city diplomas. (Actually one is not exchanged for the other, the person with an equivalency gets a city diploma in addition if he applies for one.) The policy was adopted by the city Board of Education in 1973. It was a point of issue for months preceding the board's approval of the policy, on a 3–2 vote. Opponents, including high-school principals, claimed that the policy would "water down" standards, undermine the schools, and encourage

Mostly what this plan would do is allow thousands of competent, responsible people to earn something they don't have and would like to obtain, whatever their reason or motivation: a diploma. If they deserve one and they can prove it, why shouldn't they have it? Who benefits by keeping diplomas from them? Are "standards" kept high and protected by reason of diplomas denied or unissued? Isn't it the function of schools to do all in their power to see to it that as many people as possible earn diplomas? Are diplomas less valuable because there are more of them? (If so, are the schools with the highest standards those with the most dropouts?) Would this take from the school the authority and responsibility to grant diplomas, and to set the requirements? Wouldn't schools be stronger social institutions if they could serve more people in this way? Is it irresponsible to suggest there ought to be more than one way to earn a diploma?

Is it responsible to insist there is, and should be, only one way?

---

dropouts. It remains to be seen how much the school system will promote the policy, which allows persons who once attended a New York City high school but dropped out and later earned a state equivalency diploma to apply for a city diploma on the basis of their earned equivalency.

PLAN X / *Bankrolled Educational Opportunity*

Of the ten specific reform ideas in this book, this is the most ambitious; it is also the most costly. The investment, however, is necessary if schools are to deliver on their promises; society as a whole would benefit immensely from it, and the investment eventually would bring fiscal (as well as educational) returns.

The idea itself is simple. Free public education through high school is the right of all citizens. Those who leave school before graduating, however, forgo their educational opportunity. In a sense, a school district prospers financially from dropouts—the more young people dropping out of school before graduating, the more educational dollars a district saves. Realistically, a district does not accrue these saved dollars in an account; what happens is that the students who stay in school reap the benefits in the form of better staff-student ratios, less crowded school facilities, a greater availability of books and other materials, all of which flow from the fact that some students have left school while others have stayed in. The question we raise is one of social fairness: In a society ostensibly based on a notion of equality of opportunity and in which social and career rewards are distributed in very large measure in response to attained formal education, is it fair for the public treasury to subsidize twelve years of free education for some citizens but not all?

If twelve years of free education is society's guarantee, doesn't society owe some education to a dropout, specifically an amount equal to the number of educational years he does not use? If he drops out after ten years, isn't he owed the equivalent of two years, whatever his reasons for leaving school, regardless of whose fault it was? Further, if persons who leave school later could claim an amount of dollars equal to their unused education, and use it (within guidelines) for education or training in line with their adult needs, would there not be benefits to society as well as to the individual, not the least of which would be substantial added tax revenues resulting from higher taxes such individuals would pay as the product of better jobs achieved with more education? The response that no one forced the dropout out of school and he or she could always go back, is less than realistic. How many people at the age of twenty-five or thirty-five can go back to school? How many want to?

However unusual the idea may seem, it does have precedent. It's nothing more, really, than a public-school application of the G.I. Bill (which has allowed tens of thousands of veterans to pursue college education). What was one of the chief arguments for enormous public subsidies for the further education of veterans? The returns to society—a better educated citizenry, enhanced social and economic opportunities for thousands of individuals, and ultimately increased tax revenues from a more highly trained (and paid) tax-paying veteran.

The same rationale applies to this plan, for Bankrolled Educational Opportunity. Dropouts are terribly costly to society. They tend to take lower-level jobs and, therefore, pay less in taxes. They are more prone to unemployment and underemployment, and therefore draw more unemployment benefits and more welfare. The less-educated tend to participate less in the democratic process—as voters, for example. Lack of education and lack of income often spell social trouble—poor housing, more crime, more city services of all kinds. Worst of all, and impossible to measure, is the spiritual depression of people who find themselves caught without hope. "Dropouts act upon their discontent and thus become visible symbols of the restiveness of youth."* Nor does the

* Sidney P. Marland, Jr., the former U.S. Commissioner of Education, in his annual report for 1971.

discontent disappear, we would add, when youthful dropouts become adults.

This plan, unlike the others, is not for a school district to undertake, but for a state.* If a state adopted this plan, this would happen:

A state, in keeping with its traditional responsibility for the free public education of its citizens, would adopt legislation guaranteeing twelve years of free education to all. The law would say basically that where a citizen does not have a diploma and has attended school less than twelve years, he or she would have set aside for his or her future educational use a sum equal to the value of his unused formal education.

The value of unused education would be computed by multiplying the number of educational years not used by the per capita cost of education prevailing in a citizen's school district at the time he or she officially leaves the school register. (If, for example, a district spends $1,000 a year on the average for high-school students, a person who leaves school after ten years would have forgone two years of high-school education computed at the rate of $1,000 per year. The total value of the individual's unused education would be $2,000.)

The law could set residency requirements, so that the state would not necessarily assume the burden of educating persons who move into the state after having gone to school elsewhere and failed to graduate. The law might be made to apply, for example, only to persons who attended school (public or private) in the state at least half their total school years. Even stricter eligibility requirements could be set, of course, all the way to

---

* Conceptually, there is no reason a school district could not adopt this idea, but it would make far more sense for this plan to be implemented at the state level, thereby allowing for one administrative apparatus, and one statewide procedure for applying for and receiving funds. A state, moreover, is far more able financially to undertake a social investment of this magnitude. Finally, it is highly appropriate that a state guarantee educational opportunity to all within its jurisdiction, since the state constitutionally is responsible for education; local school districts are extensions of the state; legally, they are agents of the state for the delivery of education services. The plan could be implemented on a national basis, much like the G.I. Bill.

having the law apply only to persons whose entire school career was in state.*

In any event, once eligibility requirements are set, the law would say that persons who have not used up their twelve years of education by attending school and getting a diploma may use the value of the unused balance for legitimate education and training by making application to the state. The law would require that applicants be beyond legal school age, and thus beyond the normal reach of special programs for dropouts and out-of-school youth, and at the age of no return generally in terms of regular schooling.

An agency of the state, most likely the state department of education, would keep account of all students who leave school before earning a diploma, based on reports from school districts, and compute the value of the unused education of each applicant for funds.

The state would place in trust, from its revenues, sufficient funds to cover the projected draw on the account during each fiscal year.

The state would establish administrative procedures for processing applications and disbursing funds, including regulations limiting the use of the funds to legitimate educational and training purposes. The regulations would permit the individual to use the funds for any educational purpose, from basic adult education and skill training to full-time study in a university. The regulations would prohibit the use of funds for noneducational purposes. Funds might be paid in units rather than as a large lump-sum payment, much as the Veterans Administration pays veterans' benefits in monthly installments, with the individual

---

* Needless to say, we do not advocate residency limitations, in view of their inherently restrictive purpose. The point we are making is that, where there is the objection that one state should not have to "pick up the tab" for the school dropouts of other states (that may not even have a policy of bankrolled educational opportunity), the objection can be met in the form of residency requirements. Ideally, of course, residency requirements should be avoided—they deny educational opportunity to people who need it. They also diminish the social benefits that accrue to the state from a more highly educated citizenry.

periodically required to submit evidence of continued enrollment in an educational program. Where there is evidence of misused funds, the low would allow the state to close the individual's account permanently and disburse no additional money to him or her.

Surely, this would be a large venture, financially and administratively, for any state, small or large. The states, however, do have large tax bases, including the unlimited potential of state income taxes; and eventually, as bankrolled education took hold and the incomes of people benefiting from it began to rise, the tax revenues of the state would reap a return on the investment. Hopefully, the plan would also contribute over time to a lessened need for other state social services, from welfare and unemployment to crime control and prevention of juvenile delinquency. It would be a large investment, to be sure; so were Social Security, the G.I. Bill, and the creation of land-grant universities, not to mention the development of the public schools themselves. In retrospect, these investments were critical, positive components in the development of the nation. The idea of guaranteeing twelve years of education to each citizen should not be written off because of high initial cost; we should not lose sight of the enormous potential social payoff.*

What is the alternative? To continue running schools that obviously don't work for large numbers of the young, who leave? To keep stigmatizing dropouts, because for many of them, in spite of all the special programs that exist, a return to regular schools is simply not feasible? To keep on telling ourselves that the schools are there, open to any dropout who wants to come back? (This, of course, doesn't make a dropout come back.) To listen to those who will say this would be a step toward vouchers, and "vouchers will destroy public education," and some of these public funds might be spent in private, church-related agencies and institutions? This plan is no more a plan for vouchers than was the G.I. Bill; it's no more a threat to public schools than the

---

* The authors currently are expanding the concept of Bankrolled Educational Opportunity into a detailed policy plan. The work is supported in part under a contract with the National Institute of Education.

G.I. Bill (which allows the student to choose his college) was a threat to public universities. As for public dollars and church-related institutions, again the G.I. Bill offers precedent. Because the veteran has the right to choose his college, many choose private ones, some of which are church-related. It's a specious argument that church-state barriers—which we happen to value highly—are any lower as the result.

The motivating purpose of the idea for bankrolled educational opportunity is to bring hope and means to people who have been failed by schools—and haven't received their fair share of free education. A person with hope, with options still open to him, is profoundly different from one with no hope and no apparent future options. As such people get help, society as a whole improves. Is that such a subversive proposition?

Common-sense reform ideas are infinite in number. Dwight Allen, former dean of the School of Education at the University of Massachusetts, gives a speech on thirty-one ways to change schools without much money or waiting for next year:

Let any student who is failing in any course be allowed to select his teachers.

Let any student with the approval of his parents propose his own set of graduation requirements and pursue this program of study, so long as school authorities approve.

Declare one school day each week for social service, so that students can do something "that counts for real" and, at the same time, return something to the community that is educating them.

Let parents tell the school the kind of report-card system they want for their children. "For those parents who are not very imaginative, you can have two or three standard systems available."

Let every teacher be eligible to propose and teach a course of his or her own choosing and design, so long as a sufficient number of students want the course.

Let students get credit for any course the school offers, not by taking the course but by demonstrating that they have learned the subject-matter content elsewhere.

Too often in the past school reformers have proposed ideas

that seem overly complicated, prohibitively costly, "radical" in their philosophy, and so they are vulnerable to attack and open to public suspicion. Fundamental, sweeping, *radical* alterations in how schools deal with and affect children are possible through common-sense reforms: This is what we have sought to show by describing ten such ideas.

The advantage of common-sense reform ideas is that, strategically, they can be raised in the public forum and appear so innocent. Who could logically object to the Birthday-Entrance Plan, or the Year-Round-Learning-Center Plan, or the Apprenticed-Learner Plan—even the plan for Bankrolled Educational Opportunity—*and* persuade us that they have the interests of children and youth at the top of their agenda? How long can objectors find fault with such ideas without having to admit that their concern is the job security and welfare of teachers, the administrative problems of administrators, or the private priorities of one or another special interest group?

If nothing else, common-sense reform ideas have the potential capacity to force those who say they favor change but really don't into the open, to strip empty rhetoric from hidden agendas. The public, at the very least, might then begin to see who is for children and who is for adults, who is for reform and who is for status quo. Any such measure of honesty that can be injected into the politics of school reform, and the public posturing that goes on while reform is debated and delayed, would be a small victory for the public, a beginning step perhaps toward serious reform.

Make Your Own Plan

These obviously are not the only ten ways to make schools work now. There no doubt are many ways; some better than these, we hope.

We invite readers to make their own plans to make schools work for the young. The specifics of a plan—as we hope we have made clear—are important only to the extent that a plan (a) is sensible and simple, (b) is not costly to do, and (c) is, by its nature, capable of undermining the status quo in schools so that schools come to be oriented to the needs of the young.

The number of plans that can be thought up is limitless. We urge the reader to design some. And we ask readers to share their plans with us. Don't think about schools as they are—think about what schools could do if common sense prevailed.

Readers may send their plans to us at the following address:

Harvey B. Scribner
School of Education
University of Massachusetts
Amherst, Mass. 01002

Part Three

THE SCHOOL
LEADERS

IT IS IRONIC and tragic that, at a time when strong reform-minded leadership is so necessary, there is so little of it inside so many schools. There are some reform leaders in the schools, but they are outnumbered by leaders who preach moderation or tell the public how successful the schools are, or simply stand aside while failure mounts. The reform-oriented school leader, willing to argue for serious changes in the face of opposition and controversy, is the exception these days. If the professional class as a whole will not welcome the kinds of reform ideas we have put forth, neither will the great majority of school leaders—not those in official positions of leadership; not those in unofficial positions of influence. There has developed a pervasive don't-rock-the-boat attitude in the schools. And the young who are being failed by their schools will continue to be failed for as long as this attitude prevails and controls.

Moderation is the dominant principle in school management now. Whatever you do, do it in moderation. Keep emotions cool. Qualify each statement. Do not place blame. Avoid direct criticism. Give the schools (and the school professionals) credit. Emphasize the positive. And keep in touch—keep in touch with your superiors; touch base with those in positions of influence; remember who has power and who does not, and be guided accordingly. Do not say anything that might lead the public to conclude that the schools are as bad as they really are, because this would impair the public's confidence in the schools.

Should a school "leader" favor reform? Yes, indeed. No one these days should be against change; change is the order of the day in all institutions. What kind of reform, then, should one favor? The quiet, uneventful kind. "This is what I would call moderate, incremental reform. . . ." In February 1973 a member of the central Board of Education of the City of New York, later to become its president, a professional in education himself, now a university teacher, told of the advantages of moderation.

A vibrant organization, similar to a living organism, must constantly change and mature at the same time that it maintains the very best of

its traditions. This is what I would call moderate, incremental reform
—one that weaves together both continuity and change . . .*

The point is indisputable. Still, how does one apply it to the
schools of New York or of any other city where uneven school
quality and widespread inequity are the dominant facts of life?
It is one thing to speak of keeping the "best" traditions, but what
of the worst? What of such traditions as tracking, competitive
testing, racial isolation, departmentalization of subject matter,
alienation of parents, bureaucracy, overprofessionalization, dis-
regard for the civil rights of students, uncreative uses of massive
resources, maldistribution of opportunity, and the fixing of blame
for student failure on family background? Are such discrimina-
tory traditions to be reformed moderately, to be eliminated in-
crementally? Is there no place in the American tradition for the
idea that discrimination demands bold corrective action? Revisionist school historians, Colin Greer among them, have told us
that urban schools have made a long habit of failing the children
of the poor, whatever their race or nationality, and that this habit
continues today in the case of blacks, Puerto Ricans and other
"immigrant" groups in urban schools.† Is this a habit to be al-

---

* Dr. Seymour P. Lachman, in an address in New York City.

† Greer's thesis in *The Great School Legend: A Revisionist Interpretation of
American Public Education* is that the story of how immigrants came to
America and made use of the public schools in their rise to middle-class status
is a legend. "Some groups," says Greer, "did better than others, and some
parts of some groups did best of all. But it has been equally true that some
groups did less well than others, and some parts of some groups did worst of
all. . . . Many millions in all ethnic groupings have suffered miserably in
America and continue to do so." Among the groups, or parts of ethnic groups,
that did comparatively well in the schools, according to Greer, are some immigrant Jews. It is Greer's thesis that there is an explanation for such success,
and that the explanation does not trace the reasons for success to the schools.
"Economic stability for the group," says Greer, "preceded its entry onto the
broader middle-class stage via education." Which is to say that the economic
success of such groups played a large role in educational achievement. According to Greer, "The correlation between school achievement and economic
status was so high that in school surveys carried out in the Midwest during
the 1920s it became necessary to separate Scandinavian-Americans from
other 'ethnic' Americans, because the school performance of their children so
outdistanced other foreign Midwest groups." Thus Greer's thesis explains and
accounts for success in the schools of the children of "farm-holding Scandi-

tered in incremental steps? How does one justify the morality of such moderation? "The truth of the matter," Dr. Lachman continued, "is that many of our radical school critics have been using words without any base in reality. . . ."

Perhaps. One wonders, by comparison, how much reality there is in the words typically used by the public schools, New York's included, in the official reports that describe how successful the schools are, how useful they are, how necessary they are—words that leave out those who fail in the schools or describe them by euphemisms. Whose words are more real? The words of official reports that paper over failure and discrimination? Or the words of the radical school critics? The impression left by Dr. Lachman is that hyperbole, exaggeration and ideological perception are faults to be found only in the radical critics. It would be hard to sell that argument to many parents of children who have been failed by public schools, for they have their own version of reality.

One of our basic problems [Dr. Lachman says] is that educational research so vital for genuine change is still so rudimentary. . . . Let us plan for the future . . . by increasing our storehouse of data and knowledge. . . . Let us attempt to perfect the art of education and perhaps even enhance it with information that might bring it yet to the beginnings of a science. Let us work ceaselessly to improve first our school children's basic knowledge, and then enter other areas of improvement. . . .

The points are less important than the values they reflect: Research; Planning; Data; Information; Science; Basic Knowledge. The values come at us as if from another time. Individually, they would not excite criticism. Collectively, they suggest an inherent conservatism and, set in the context of an assault on "radical" reform, they suggest a reactionary bent.

---

navians and storekeeping Jews," as well as the children of economically stable Greek and Japanese immigrants. The Greer argument could be applied, it would seem, to such other groups as the Chinese immigrants of New York City.

The invocation of "Research" sounds so reasonable and authentically academic, and it serves to justify inaction while we wait for the results of research that may never be undertaken. "Planning" sounds so professional, so necessary, and would seem to assure the certainty that "radicals" never guarantee. "Data" and "Information" are the tools of rational decision-makers and goal-oriented managers. "Science"—to transform education into a science is the classic goal of professional and parent alike. The professional for reasons of status, the parent for reasons of formula-guaranteed education. "Basic Knowledge"—who would argue that literacy is the highest priority? But here, in this particular series of values, there is an implied message, which is that "incremental" reformers remember this priority while "radical" reformers tend to lose sight of it in their preoccupation with criticism.

. . . and let us always be proud [Dr. Lachman concludes] to be known as moderate and incremental reformers trying hard to improve a school system without destroying it in the process.*

The message is clear: Nothing basic is wrong. Have patience. The bugs in the system ultimately will be refined out. It reminds us of the comment by Peter Schrag, the social critic, that the worst attribute of schools is not their capacity to fail so many of the young, "but their refusal to produce honest data on that failure."† Thus failure is papered over. Thus corrective action is impossible. So it is with regard to reform. If it is bad that schools have been unable thus far to reform themselves for the sake of the young, it is worse that their leaders fail even to see the need for serious reforms.

* For reasons that should be obvious, the speech by Dr. Lachman was praised by Albert Shanker, who devoted one of his weekly advertisements in the *Sunday New York Times* to a report on it. In Mr. Shanker's view, Dr. Lachman's comments should "serve as a guideline for all who are seriously committed to the search for valid answers to our schools' problems and to the larger task of restoring full effectiveness, harmony and dignity to New York's school system."

† Peter Schrag, *Out of Place in America*.

Cautiousness dominates public education these days. Federal leadership seems more concerned with research than with equality. The funding agents in the foundations and in the government, pressed by a faltering economy and a political backlash, seem sensitive to the political implications of where their grant money goes and what it buys. Not all, but the majority of school administrators have virtually gone underground; jobs are scarce, and there is more concern for job security than at any time in recent memory. Professionals in general are everywhere conscious of tenure, retention rights, severance policies, pensions, promotional opportunities, and keeping the gates to the profession as closed as possible so that competition for jobs does not worsen an already bad situation. There are exceptions, as always.

There are those who contend that the public schools are more attuned to reform now than at any point in the history of public education, but that funds for new projects have dried up. Still others contend that the schools are in the midst of a quiet reformation.

There is some evidence to support these contentions. The public schools of America do continue to "experiment" and "innovate." They continue to speak of turning the corner on student underachievement. They continue to account for an impressive percentage of the gross national product. New school buildings— symbols of institutional vigor—continue to be built despite periodic taxpayer revolts against spending for public education. One can discern an emerging "Right to Read" program which the federal government, in a fit of idealism, began as a national crusade against illiteracy. There is one movement underway to mass-produce competency in teaching, and a second movement, not unrelated, to make schools more accountable to the public. Parents and students, often with the help of attorneys and advocacy groups, have gained new rights of participation in some areas of school decision-making. In more than a few states, major fiscal renovations are underway that would more equally balance school spending—and hopefully school quality—across local school districts. Most striking of all, the notion of "alternatives" in education has taken root in the public schools. From New York City to Berkeley, from Minneapolis to Kentucky, there are scores of public schools that call themselves "alternative schools," and such words as "alternatives" and "options," which originated in the demands of school critics, have been incorporated into the vocabularies of public-school administrators, and into the language of official school documents as well.

Still, despite all this, the atmosphere has changed; one cannot shake the general impression. On one morning in February 1974 the *Boston Globe* published, side by side, two articles on schools. The subject was racial integration. The first article informed us that according to documents just made public the federal government in 1962 nearly shut off federal funds to Mississippi as part of the administration's pressure to desegregate schools. The second article spelled out the court's move to block integration in the schools of Detroit. In a decade, the sense of the government and the people it represents seems to have come full circle, from pro-integration to anti-integration.

In the public schools, where leaders a decade ago spoke forcefully and frequently for "quality integrated education," there is silence; integration is a high-risk issue, and few school leaders today are willing to be caught standing unequivocally for it in public. Where there used to be agonizing over school dropouts, now comes a National Commission on the Reform of Secondary Education recommending that students be allowed to leave school at the age of fourteen, two years earlier than most states presently allow, on the ground that "forced schooling" is "the foremost problem in American education." One wonders to whom the Commission spoke. Did the people who live in the central Harlems and the Appalachias—"the other America," as Michael Harrington called it—say that "forced schooling" is the "foremost problem" with their schools? Did they say that if their fourteen-year-old sons and daughters were allowed to leave school their lives would be enhanced? Did the Commission not see that noncompulsory education requires a positive alternative, a place to go; and that lacking a place to go, the kind of recommendation it put forth likely would not liberate the young, but would free the schools to rid themselves systematically and legally of the particularly "troublesome" students who learn slowly or behave badly —the "dull" and the "maladjusted" who "get in the way" of the majority?

In New York City, the public schools announce that henceforth children will be promoted from grade to grade only if they achieve specified reading levels; those who perform below the standards will be held back. Thus is the reading problem "solved," and thus are "standards" guaranteed in the nation's pre-eminent school system. Were those who devised this policy concerned with helping children learn to read? Or were they more concerned with their public image as standard-setters? Where is the research that says children who "stay back" a grade will improve their reading skills? Is this policy any less defeating than a policy of automatic promotion from grade to grade regardless of ability? Is not the real issue the delivery of help to children regardless of grade level? What guarantee do schools make to the child that a first-rate teacher will be provided? How will a policy that keeps a child back help the child to get the help that is needed? Why do we have to hold children back to get them help in learning to read?

The behavior of school administrators—not all, but most—has changed markedly in a decade. (Not unlike the dramatic transformation that took place in national politics over the same period.) Ten years ago the issues of urgency in education were human in nature—equality, integration, fair treatment of children, students' rights, equity. And the sharp, moral commitment to social justice of the highest leaders—Keppel, Howe and Allen* are examples—reflected throughout the schools. Today the issues of concern in most of the places where schools are administered are less human than institutional: finance, organization, management, objectives, efficiency, fiscal accounting. And the schools look for, and get, "good administrators"—low-profile, dispassionate, thoroughly professionalized administrators, who will keep the schools

* The reference is to three former U.S. Commissioners of Education: Francis Keppel, Harold Howe, and the late James Allen, who achieved a national reputation while Commissioner of Education for the State of New York.

running, keep the staff content, keep parents in hand, and keep students under control. Moderation, consensus, compromise—these are the most visible values in the administration of most schools these days. It reminds us of a description of "survivalist" leadership, where the object is

to hang on to as much of the past as possible, to avoid trouble, to follow the political adage of the Third Republic in France that you can survive in public office provided you do nothing. . . . To take no risks, to assume a posture of low visibility, to say nothing but to say it well. . . . The graceful protection of the status quo is the course of action for survival.*

There are two school systems in America. There is the successful system that most Americans think they know, populated by the children who succeed, as described in the official reports of the schools, as alluded to in the statements of school boards and school administrators, and as imprinted in the memory of much of middle-class adult America. This is the system that tradition tells us helped to form America, that helps to keep it strong and secure, and that provides unlimited opportunity to those who can benefit from school and who are interested in education. In this system the schools work for the young: this is the universal system of public education whose development has been traced and whose social benefits have been praised by (among many others) President Lawrence A. Cremin, of Teachers College, Columbia University.†

The second school system is less visible in a time when it is popular not to see failure. The students of this system do poorly in school. Typically, the longer they stay in school the worse they do. In this system, the young learn to dislike schools and books. This is a system of boredom, frustration, listlessness, tension, misbehavior and, frequently, crime. The "graduates" of this system fill the ranks of the adult unemployed and underemployed.

* From *Priorities for Action: Final Report of the Carnegie Commission on Higher Education,* 1973.
† See his *The Transformation of the School,* 1961; and *The Genius of American Education,* 1965.

They account for many of the government statistics on low income and welfare. They live on the fringes of society.

The "graduates" of the second system rarely hold a grudge against the schools that have failed them. Not long ago a mother came to one of us and told about her son. At age eight her boy was in the third grade, and the school had advised the family that because he was not reading well enough it was likely that he would "stay back" in the coming school year. This boy was of normal intelligence, attended school regularly and was well-behaved; he simply had a problem with reading, and his school —as the great majority of schools would do—perceived the problem as the boy's fault. He would be held back one year to try to overcome his problem. The mother was disappointed and concerned, but she did not intend to complain. Without being conscious of it, she seemed to know that there are two school systems—one for those who succeed and one for those who fail —and that her son was about to enter the second system. If he follows the pattern that thousands of other children have established before him, it is unlikely that he will emerge from that system until he has learned to dislike school and detest learning.

More than a decade ago Michael Harrington wrote of the two Americas—the "familiar" America with "the highest mass standard of living the world has ever known," and "the other America" of poverty. One America is easily seen; the other is invisible, and it is Harrington's conclusion that until the poor America becomes visible—which is to say that until the comfortable America chooses to see the poor America—little can be done to make the inhabitants of "the other America" less poor. That was 1962. Thirteen years later, Harrington's description is not outdated.

In the schools of America there is a similar parallelism. And there is little desire either by professionals or by the public at large to see the second system, or to see that moderation and the illusion of well-being will go a long way toward keeping the second system intact and out of public view.

These are the figures [Harrington wrote, after reciting the statistics of poverty], and there is legitimate reason for sincere men to argue over the details, to claim that a particular interpretation is too high or too low. At this point I would beg the reader to forget the numbers game. Whatever the precise calibrations, it is obvious that these statistics represent an enormous, an unconscionable amount of human suffering in this land. They should be read with a sense of outrage. For until these facts shame us, until they stir us to action, the other America will continue to exist, a monstrous example of needless suffering in the most advanced society in the world.[*]

Early in 1970 the New York City schools published its own brief description of the public schools of the City of New York. The booklet itemized the services and the scope of the system: more than 900 schools; more than 1.1 million students; more than 110,000 employees, the majority of them professionals; health and guidance services; special schools and services for the handicapped and the emotionally disturbed; subsidized lunches for the poor; educational television; evening schools and summer schools; schools for adults and out-of-school youth; special projects for special purposes funded by Washington or Albany; experiments; computerized programming; innovation; new schools. The portrait was impressive.

In the same year a citizen organization[†] issued a second report on the New York schools. Whereas the official report described the "familiar" school system, this second report described the "other" system. It spoke of "an increasing estrangement between students and faculty," of "a mutual distrust between student and teacher," and of hidden failure by staggering numbers of high-school students. A total of 65,203 students entered the high schools of New York as the class of 1968, the report said. Four years later, when the class of '68 graduated, more than 25,000 of them had disappeared; they had dropped out, moved out, transferred, or been dropped from the schools' rolls for one reason or another. The schools did not know where they had gone. The missing represented 39.5 percent of the original class. In addition, the report continued, another 15,603 students who

[*] Michael Harrington, *The Other America.*
[†] The Citizens' Committee for Children of New York, Inc. The report is "A Report on New York City High Schools," January 5, 1970.

did graduate with the class of '68 received "general" diplomas, the least desirable and least useful of several kinds of diplomas that the city's high schools awarded.* A "general" diploma; this report said, "is a euphemism which can be taken as meaning that the children got their bodies to school and kept them there most of the time. It does not mean that they were touched and taught by our schools." The holder of a general diploma, it was said, was little better off than a dropout with no diploma. Taken together, the "missing" and the recipients of general diplomas accounted for 63.4 percent of the original class of '68. In numbers, they accounted for approximately 40,000 youth.

One cannot reasonably expect the schools of New York or any other major city to cure massive, complex inequities overnight. But one must expect at least that they will recognize the problem. Tragically, there is little desire to see the problems, just as there is little desire on the part of the nation to look at its own poverty.

In most cities there is visible concern with crime in the schools, with the protection of school jobs, with finding the money necessary to keep schools open and running, with negotiating labor contracts, and with balancing the budget. Such concerns are legitimate. Unfortunately, they consume virtually all the attention of the school system and the interested public, to the near exclusion of concern for the more fundamental problem—the continuing existence of two school systems. The fact is that when school crime is eliminated, when jobs are distributed, when the needed money is found, after the contracts are agreed upon, and after the budgets are balanced, the other school system of failure will still be there.

"Until these facts shame us . . ." If one third of the lights in New York City went off, if one third of the subway system stopped running, if one third of the stores decided to leave the city, there would be a public uproar and massive official action.

---

* The school system has since abolished the multiple-diploma system. It now awards a single diploma to all graduates. The change was vehemently opposed by many parents and many high school principals who asserted that the change would result in the "watering down" of standards.

When one third (or more) of the city's high-school students are lost during the process of education, we are advised by leaders of prominence—by leaders of the Board of Education and the city's school professionals—that the critics have bad vision, that the schools are basically well, and that the road to better schools is paved with moderate, incremental reform.

Part Four

THE HOPE

What is the hope for school reform? Is reform possible any more?

Ivan Illich* says that we should not waste time hoping (or working) for the reform of schools. Instead we should get on with the business of abolishing them. Schools are empty of education, full of ritual, his argument goes. Therefore, for the sake of the young and a better society, schools should be disestablished. No more compulsory education. No more formal education. Ban the diploma. Prohibit discrimination on the basis of accumulated education. Create informal networks, and share our skills and knowledge by mutual consent and for mutual benefit. The Illich vision is of a deschooled society.

The Illich critique of schooling and the way credentials are offered is incisive and on target, but its ultimate conclusion is not persuasive. Schools may be places of empty ritual, but it is difficult to generate much hope that informal "learning webs" would not be susceptible to comparable ills, not least of which might be their domination by established elites, professional or otherwise. Diplomas, degrees and other credentials may be means of discriminating, but it is reasonable that their elimination would be followed quickly by the creation of other instruments of marking and sorting people; schools may justify class systems, but they did not create them. The problems of the world are mostly other than educational—hunger, violence, tyranny, prejudice, poverty. It is difficult to envision how such problems would recede if schools were disestablished; it is easy to foresee things getting even worse. The Illich theory fails to answer two basic questions: In what ways would the world be a better place without schools? How would the young be better off?

A second and more important critic, Charles E. Silberman,† has another view of schools and school reform. The hope, he says, is to recognize that schools do not have to be bad. The cause of bad schools is "mindlessness," his theory goes, and when

* See his *Deschooling Society.*
† Author of *Crisis in the Classroom: The Remaking of American Education.*

schools are bad, two sets of people get hurt: the children and the
teachers. The Silberman critique of schools rests in part on this
teacher-as-victim concept. School reform thus has two outcomes:
the liberation of teachers, and the improvement of educational
opportunities for the young.

Silberman is not the usual critic; he likes teachers. "To read
some of the more important and influential contemporary critics
of education—men like Edgar Friedenberg, Paul Goodman, John
Holt, Jonathan Kozol—one might think that the schools are
staffed by sadists and clods," Silberman wrote in *Crisis in the
Classroom,* an enormously popular and widely praised book.*

But teachers *are* human. . . . If they appear otherwise, it is because the institution in which they are engulfed demands it of them.
. . . If placed in an atmosphere of freedom and trust, if treated as
professionals and as people of worth, teachers behave like the caring,
concerned people they would like to be. They, no less than their students, are victimized by the way in which schools are currently organized and run.

There are an enormous number of decent, capable professionals
in the schools of America. They exist in virtually every school.
And the best are, as Silberman says, crushed or chased away by
the worst of schools, the worst of administrators, and the prolif-
eration of petty rules.

The explanation, however, is incomplete. The trouble with
Silberman's explanation is that it falls short of the entire story,
and what is omitted is at least as significant as what is there. If
most teachers are "decent, honest, well-intentioned people" with
an inherent concern for the young, one must presume that they
are also reasonably intelligent, reasonably skilled and endowed
with a certain amount of perception. And if so many schools are

---

* The book, among its other awards, received the John Dewey Award of
the United Federation of Teachers of New York City. The empathy of Mr.
Silberman for teachers no doubt was a major factor, since teachers have been
notably negative toward other critics of schools. The acceptability of *Crisis in
the Classroom* is one feature that distinguishes it from the rest of the body of
literature that criticizes schools and schooling—the book was acceptable to
professional and layman alike.

so badly run that they victimize teacher and student alike, the question is: What are the teachers doing about the bad situation? Are teachers so intimidated and controlled by their supervisors and principals that they are fearful to lift a finger in protest? Have teachers come to feel that it is not their place to question school practices that they view as harmful to children? Why aren't more teachers in revolt against repressive schools and incompetent principals? Why aren't more teachers allied with students and parents in protesting inequitable policies and unjust rules? Why do so many teachers speak of "my children"—but do not speak up against schools that they must know are numbing so many of the young? We recall the comment Archibald Cox made about the many fine young men in Washington who found it impossible to say No to their superiors in the Watergate era. One wonders how many fine men and women are teaching in schools that are harming students—and failing to speak or act against the harm they see. The Silberman explanation seems to imply that teachers have no capacity to take a stand to protect the young.

The Silberman theory of teachers as powerless victims of bad schools also falls short of reality in a second respect—its failure to recognize the power of organized teachers, and to analyze the ends toward which this power more than occasionally is used. Teacher organizations frequently oppose reforms that might improve schools and would help children. During our time in New York City, the United Federation of Teachers fought against decentralization of the school system, opposed expansion of teacher licenses for bilingual teachers, opposed efforts to liberalize the licensing system for teachers and other professionals; and worked in the state legislature for bills to restrict the counseling of students to licensed guidance counselors (and thereby prevent classroom teachers from counseling students), to impair reorganization of the central school headquarters by mandating retention of several powerful central bureaus. During the same time, organized teachers opposed state legislation to permit commercial driving schools to teach students how to drive, to establish parent councils with the right to observe teachers in the classroom, to allow schools to be open on weekends, to make teacher tenure subject to periodic renewal.

The Silberman thesis stops short of the more abrasive conclusion that teachers do have to bear some of the responsibility for bad schools—to the extent, first, that they may fail as individuals; but more to the extent, second, that they allow their organizations, union or otherwise, to work politically to block and impair school reforms. Do the medical professions have a responsibility to help make the nation's health-care systems more rational and more equitable? Have they had no political role in blocking or slowing down reformist proposals?

Charles Silberman is not an apologist for bad schools; he is an extremely important advocate of better schools, and he has added his considerable weight to the task of school reform. Nor, as should be equally needless to say, do we subscribe to any brief that would diminish the right of teachers to organize, lobby, campaign and bargain, to influence public opinion, and take stands on matters of public importance, including the endorsing of candidates for public office. But Silberman's critique, valuable for its vision of schools as humane institutions in a humane society, puts them in a political vacuum. They are not, and never have been. Silberman tells us little about the politics of reforming schools; and without such an understanding, schools are not likely to be changed very much.

A third critic, Mario D. Fantini,* has looked at school reform and emerged with an attractive concept—"public schools of choice." Families would select the kind of schools they want for their children. It is a kind of voucher system. But is it realistic to believe that, as Fantini says, this sweeping reform can come about through "a politics of cooperation" that brings together "the thousands of people of good will, both in and out of our public schools, who are really motivated by what is best for chil-

* Author of *Public Schools of Choice: A Plan for the Reform of American Education.* We urge its readers to give special attention to the book's appendix, which contains an exchange between Fantini and Herb Kohl, a rather well-known school critic. It is a revealing exchange on the politics of school reform.

dren?" And can we believe that such an ambitious plan for the refashioning of American education could be achieved without a real loss of power for professionals and a commensurate gain for parents in such matters as control, governance and prerogative?

Fantini's dream is this: "Teachers, students, parents, administrators can work together if they feel that their own rights are not being preempted." But is it not precisely the point that some existing "rights" will have to be "preempted" if a system that now withholds power and influence from parents and the young is to be made over? Can there be "public schools of choice" without changing most if not virtually all existing ways of conducting school business? Would this not preempt or revise many prerogatives that professionals now enjoy? What serious reforms can these people of good will discuss, plan and implement which do not preempt someone's "rights?" Where a "right" would be preempted, would this mean the plan in question would be scrapped so that no one of good will would be offended and walk away? Is this not a formula for no reform, or reform only of the harmless variety to which no one of consequence would object?

Fantini concedes that his notion of cooperative politics "may appear to be naïve." We are forced to agree, even though we are attracted to his schools of choice. It is not merely a matter of separating those of good will from those of ill will. The problem is that professionals of good will have their own agenda to follow. That agenda, rhetoric aside, takes precedence over the reforming of schools; indeed, it often conflicts with reform ideas.

What, then, is the hope, what is the strategy of reform? No one can imagine the shapes and forms that schools and education will take in a generation. But there are some goals that we should be heading for.

We can assume that such areas as how schools are organized, how they are governed, whom they employ, how students enter and leave and re-enter, how education is defined, how opportunities are guaranteed will be subjects of debate, and should be targets of reform. We should strive for flexibility of policies, in contrast to policies that restrict and contain.

We can assume, given the new legitimacy of pluralism, that diversity will be a powerful theme in future educational policy. We should work to increase the interest in alternatives in education—specifically, alternatives within the public-education sector. The demand for choices has already begun to make itself felt. The notion of "public schools of choice" would have been unthinkable just a few years ago; now the idea is taken seriously. We should encourage the trend to deliberately send students out of school for the sake of their education—into internships, apprenticeships, work-study, "city as school" and "parkway" programs—and push it downward to include younger children. We can assume that the education of parents and other adults will be of more concern, not less. The wildest schemes we can dream up now may seem quaintly conventional before the turn of the century. We should look for policies that encourage the creation of "wild" schemes, and give them the chance to be tried. The greater risk is to do only that which is safe.

We can assume, and hope, that the public will insist on more direct accountability from its schools, and that parents will demand more of a direct role in the governing of schools. We can assume that professionals will not take the parents' challenge lightly. Indications are that the public treasury will be less able to give schools all the money they say they need. And because parents and legislators will demand more concrete evidence of results, schools will seemingly be in the position of being asked to do more with less. It's not an altogether unreasonable demand, given the historical reticence and inability of schools to close out failing efforts as a way of saving money for promising ideas. But schools and school leaders will tend to see it that way.*

Are schools preparing for the future? Are they asking questions of fundamental consequence to the lives of the young? Are they consciously making themselves more flexible institutions—questioning old practices, looking with honest skepticism on old re-

---

* We hope it is clear that we are not suggesting that public education ought to get less financial support. It ought to get more. The point is that money alone, without serious reforms, will not make schools that are worthy of the young.

straints and old limits, reaching out for parents, stretching old definitions of education, taking down old barriers between home and school and classroom and world, asking the universities for assistance in the creative design of new visions of school? As they build each new annual budget, do they weigh the existing ways of spending money with the same scrutiny that is given to proposed new ways? Are they restudying the words and recommendations of their critics in search of clues as to how they might relate more productively with students and parents, and teachers as well? We leave it to parents to judge their own schools. By our standard of judgment, the great majority of schools—though there are notable, refreshing, exciting exceptions—cannot see the future yet, because they are looking behind.

The hope for the reform of the public schools rests with the public, especially parents.* Parents must believe they are capable of governing schools, able to select teachers and principals, worthy of making the decisions as to how their children will be educated. Parents have been trained that it is not their place to question educational practice, that it is inappropriate for them to be critical and discontented. The role of the good parent is

* Throughout this book we have argued for parent participation in the control of schools. The conservatism and traditionalism inherent in the views of a great many parents do not dissuade us from this basic recommendation. The public, we feel, has been taught to think about schools in traditional, conservative, uncreative ways by school leaders who, over the years, have tended to be conservative, traditional and professional-oriented themselves. With little opportunity to participate in educational planning and decision-making, the public has little reason, indeed, not to believe what it is told. We would submit that the more the leaders in education talk about the need for more professionals, more new buildings, more discipline, separate schools for "disruptive" children, the dangers of "radical" reforms, et cetera, the more the public will reflect these opinions in the polls that ask the public what it thinks about schools. Further, we would submit that the more parents and other citizens participate directly and consistently in school decision-making, the more they will be exposed to the failure that goes on in the name of education, the more they will make their own conclusions as to causes and solutions, and the more the public's opinions on schools will become enlightened and creative. The great majority of parents, schooled and unschooled, are reasonable, intelligent people who want their schools to serve their children. It is our belief that the more they learn at first hand about schools the more they will demand very serious reforms.

part of the legend: to be supportive, to be helpful, to rally other taxpayers in support of schools, to belong to the P.T.A., to make sure the young stay in school, to come to graduation ceremonies. Parents have yet to take their ultimate role, their ultimate responsibility: to control their schools as a piece of their government.

The day will come, we hope, in some communities, small and large, when parents will say to the professionals they employ, "This is what we want for our children. Don't tell us the reasons it can't be done. Tell us how to do it. Or give us a better idea." Should the school board choose to respond that the parents' wishes cannot be fulfilled, because of this contract or that understanding, because of this policy or that regulation, and indicate its unwillingness to act, the parents at least will know where the problem is. They will know that they are not as represented as they may have thought. They will know, too, that their rights and their children's rights have been bargained or given away by their own representatives.

How refreshing it would be to see families picking and choosing the days on which they send their children to school, days that make sense to them and fit the family schedule; to see children treated and learning as individuals, each following a personally tailored program of study; to see older children and young adults of high-school age systematically guided by their schools into educational work experience, internships, apprenticeships, community service and research, all outside the walls of the school; to see all students of all ages paired for regular periods of tutoring and mutual aid; to hear students and their parents intelligently discussing which teachers to select in the coming session, knowing that the choice is theirs; to watch boards of education discovering human-size space for learning in vacant houses and commercial buildings, and lease it instead of building yet another massive schoolhouse; to witness, perhaps, an intensely troubled urban high school making sensible plans for its own renewal and reorganization by taking the risk of stopping classes while students and teachers work together on a plan; to find parents of each school electing their own governing boards to control their school; to read in the newspaper a routine announcement of diplomas awarded to persons long past school age, on the basis of competence acquired and demonstrated external to schools; to see a state guarantee twelve years of education to all its citizens, including those who "save" some of their allotted years for later in life.

If the class of professionals has higher priorities than reform, if school boards tend to be less than aggressive in protecting the public's interests and in representing the young who but the parent can be expected to take the lead in the reformation of schools? Who is more appropriate to lead? At the bottom line the citizenry is responsible for its own institutions; and the public, when aroused and informed, has a powerful reform capacity, far transcending that of professionals, school boards, or even critics.

This is the hope: that the public will become aroused and enlightened and that their necessary leadership will come forth. This would be the first step toward creating systems of public education that are worthy of the young. Difficult as it may be, the first step could prove to be nine tenths of the journey.

Reading List

By no means is this an all-inclusive list of works in the field of school reform, school policy and school politics; it is a list of references that we have found especially useful to us in our work in this field. We have included most of the standard contemporary works on school criticism and school reform; we have made a special effort, however, to list books, articles and documents that have been less widely publicized, in the hope that some readers will find this of use. The list does not include works that focus on "open" or "informal" education; that is a field of its own.

Allen, Dwight, and Hecht, Jeffrey, eds., *Controversies in Education,* Saunders, 1974.

Ashton-Warner, Sylvia, *Teacher,* Simon and Schuster, 1963.

Bailey, Stephen K., *Disruption in Urban Public Secondary Schools,* National Association of Secondary School Principals, 1970.

Board of Education, City of New York, *Parent Associations and the Schools,* 1971.

————, *Regulations Governing the Collection, Maintenance and Dissemination of Student Records,* 1973.

————, *Requirements for the High School Diploma* (including regulations whereby holders of equivalency diplomas may obtain in addition a New York City diploma), 1973.

————, *Student Rights and Responsibilities,* 1970.

Bowles, Samuel, and Gintis, Herbert, *Nightmares and Dreams: Capitalism and Education in the United States,* manuscript scheduled for publication by Harper and Row in 1975.

Boocock, Sarane S., *An Introduction to the Sociology of Learning,* Houghton Mifflin, 1972.

Braun, Robert J., *Teachers and Power,* Simon and Schuster, 1972.

Bremer, John, and von Moschzisker, Michael, *The School Without Walls: Philadelphia's Parkway Program,* Holt, Rinehart and Winston, 1971.

Bronfenbrenner, Urie, *Two Worlds of Childhood,* Simon and Schuster, (Touchstone), 1972.

Carnegie Commission on Higher Education, *Priorities for Action: Final Report of the Carnegie Commission on Higher Education,* McGraw-Hill, 1973.

Center for Law and Education, Harvard University, *Inequality in Education,* published quarterly.

Center for Research and Education in American Liberties, Columbia University and Teachers College, *Civic Education in a Crisis Age: An Alternative to Repression and Revolution,* Introduction by Alan F. Westin; summary of a research project to develop objectives for a new civic education curriculum for American secondary schools in the 1970s, September 1970.

Channon, Gloria, *Homework!* Outerbridge & Dienstfrey, 1970.

Clark, Kenneth, *Dark Ghetto,* Harper and Row, 1965.

Danforth Foundation and the Ford Foundation, *The School and the Democratic Environment,* Columbia University Press, 1970.

Dennison, George, *The Lives of Children,* Random House, 1969.

Educational Facilities Laboratories, *Schools: More Space/Less Money,* 1971. E.F.L. regularly publishes documents and reports of interest to persons with a concern for imaginative ways to create and use space for learning.

Educational Facilities Laboratories, *Urban Educational Facilities Options: The Final Report of the New York City School Space Study Committee* (Mimeographed), 1972.

Fantini, Mario, *Public Schools of Choice: A Plan for the Reform of American Education,* Simon and Schuster, 1973. See especially the appendix, an exchange of commentaries between Fantini and Herbert Kohl.

Ford Foundation, *A Foundation Goes to School,* 1972.

Friedenberg, Edgar, *Coming of Age in America,* Random House (Vintage paperback), 1963.

———, *The Vanishing Adolescent,* Dell (paperback), 1959.

Gartner, Alan; Koehler, Mary; and Riessman, Frank, *Children Teach Children: Learning by Teaching,* Harper & Row, 1971.

Gattegno, Caleb. *What We Owe Children: The Subordination of Teaching to Learning,* Outerbridge & Dienstfrey, 1970.

Goodman, Paul, *Compulsory Mis-education and the Community of Scholars,* Vintage, 1962.

———, *Growing Up Absurd,* Vintage, 1956.

Graubard, Allen, *Free the Children: Radical Reform and the Free School Movement,* Pantheon, 1972.

Greer, Colin, *The Great School Legend: A Revisionist Interpretation of American Public Education,* Basic Books, 1972.

————, ed., *The Solution as Part of the Problem*, Harper & Row. 1973.

Gross, Ronald, and Gross, Beatrice, eds., *Radical School Reform*, Simon and Schuster, 1969.

Gross, Ronald, and Osterman, Paul, eds., *High School*, Simon and Schuster (Touchstone), 1972.

Harrington, Michael, *The Other America*, Pelican Books, revised edition, 1971.

Hentoff, Nat, *Our Children Are Dying*, Viking, 1967.

Herndon, James, *How to Survive in Your Native Land*, Simon and Schuster, 1971.

————, *The Way It Spozed to Be*, Simon and Schuster, 1968, Bantam Books, 1968.

Hersey, John, *Letter to the Alumni*, Alfred A. Knopf, 1970.

Holt, John, *How Children Fail*, Dell, 1964.

————, *How Children Learn*, Pitman, 1967.

————, *The Underachieving School*, Pitman, 1969.

————, *What Do I Do Monday?* Dutton, 1970.

Illich, Ivan, *Deschooling Society*, Harper & Row, 1971.

Jencks, Christopher, *et al.*, *Inequality: A Reassessment of the Effect of Family and Schooling in America*, Basic Books, 1972.

Katz, Michael B., ed., *Class, Bureaucracy and Schools: The Illusion of Educational Change in America*, Praeger, 1971.

————, *School Reform: Past and Present*, Little, Brown, 1971.

Kohl, Herbert, *The Open Classroom*, The New York Review, 1969.

————, *Reading, How to*, Dutton, 1973.

————, *Teaching the Unteachable*, The New York Review, 1967.

————, *36 Children*, New American Library, 1967.

Kotler, Milton, *Neighborhood Government: The Local Foundations of Political Life*, Bobbs-Merrill, 1969.

Kozol, Jonathan, *Death at an Early Age*, Houghton Mifflin, 1967.

————, *Free Schools*, Houghton Mifflin, 1972.

Lurie, Ellen. *How to Change the Schools: A Parents' Action Handbook on How to Fight the System*, Random House, 1970.

Massachusetts Advocacy Center/Massachusetts Law Reform Institute, *Making School Work: An Education Handbook for Students, Parents and Professionals*, 1973.

Metropolitan Applied Research Center, *Fact Book on Pupil Transportation*, MARC Document Nr. 2, 1972.

Mosteller, Frederick, and Moynihan, Daniel P., eds., *On Equality of Educational Opportunity: Papers Deriving from the Harvard University Faculty Seminar on the Coleman Report*, Vintage Books, 1972.

N.A.A.C.P. Legal Defense and Educational Fund, Inc., *It's Not the*

Distance, "It's the Niggers," comments on the controversy over school busing, May 1972.

New York State Commission on the Quality, Cost and Financing of Elementary and Secondary Education. Commission reports are contained in volumes published during 1972.

Postman, Neil, and Weingartner, Charles, *Teaching as a Subversive Activity,* Delacorte Press, 1969.

Public Education Association (of New York City), *Equal Employment Opportunities and the New York City Public Schools: An Analysis and Recommendations based on Public Hearings Held January 25-29, 1971, by the City of New York Commission on Human Rights,* 1971.

Rebell, Michael A., "New York's School Decentralization Law: Two and a Half Years Later," *Journal of Law and Education,* January 1973.

Reimer, Everett, *An Essay on Alternatives in Education,* Centro Intercultural de Documentación, Cuernavaca, Mexico, 1970.

Rogers, David, *The Management of Big Cities: Interest Groups and Social Change Strategies,* Sage Publications, 1971.

————, *110 Livingston Street: Politics and Bureaucracy in the New York City School System,* Random House, 1968.

Rothman, Esther, *The Angel Inside Went Sour,* McKay, 1970.

Schoolboys of Barbiana, *Letter to a Teacher,* Random House, 1970.

Schrag, Peter. *Village School Downtown,* Beacon Press, 1967.

————, *Voices in the Classroom,* Beacon Press, 1965.

Schultz, Stanley K., *The Culture Factory,* Oxford University Press, 1973.

Scribner, Harvey, and Stevens, Leonard, "The Politics of Teacher Competence," *Phi Delta Kappan,* September 1974.

Sexton, Patricia C., ed., *School Policy and Issues in a Changing Society,* Allyn and Bacon, 1971.

Silberman, Charles, *Crisis in the Classroom: The Remaking of American Education,* Random House, 1970.

State of New York, Office of Education Performance Review, *School Factors Influencing Reading Achievement: A Case Study of Two Inner City Schools,* March 1974.

Stevens, Leonard, *Alternative Education within the Public Schools,* Croft Educational Services Inc., Croft Leadership Action Folio Nr. 59, 1973.

Study Commission on Undergraduate Education and the Education of Teachers, *The University Can't Train Teachers,* 1971.

Toffler, Alvin, *Future Shock,* Random House, 1970.

Tractenberg, Paul, *Testing the Teacher: How Urban School Districts*

Select Their Teachers and Supervisors, foreword by Eleanor Holmes Norton, Agathon Press, 1974.

United States Department of Health, Education and Welfare. *Report on Higher Education*—report of a task force headed by Frank Newman, 1971.

University of the State of New York/New York State Department of Education, *Guidelines for Students' Rights and Responsibilities,* 1972.

Urban Education Task Force of the Department of Health, Education and Welfare, *The Urban Education Task Force Report,* Praeger, 1970.

Vermont Department of Education. *Vermont Design for Education,* 1969.

Wasserman, Miriam, *The School Fix, NYC, USA,* Simon and Schuster (A Clarion Book), 1971.

Wasserman, Miriam, ed., *Demystifying School,* Praeger, 1974.

Wittes, Simon, *People and Power: A Study of Crisis in Secondary Schools,* University of Michigan, 1970.

Index

Abolition of schools, 117
Academic credit, apprenticeships
    and, 47–48
Accountability, 107, 122
    committee of, 16n.
    most-wanted-teacher plan and,
        45
Administrators
    apprenticeships and, 48
    changing behavior of, 109–10
    moderation of, 103–5, 106
    renewal plan and, 68, 69, 70
Advisers, planning and, 69, 72
After-school programs, retention
    rights and, 15, 16
Allen, Dwight, 98
Allen, James, 109n.
Alternative schools, 108
Alternatives in education, 122
American Federation of Teach-
    ers, 14n.
Antipoverty program, tutoring
    in, 52
Apprenticed-learner plan, 46–50
    academic credit and, 47–48
    administrators and, 48
    advantages of, 49–50
    contracts for, 47
    legislation for, 50
    personnel for, 47
    workability of, 49

Assignment of students, 43
Assistants, teacher, 41, 42
Autonomous-school plan, 76–85
    budget and, 80
    decision-making and, 78
    district school board and, 79,
        80
    draft plan for, 79
    election of governing body for,
        80
    evaluation and, 80, 81, 84
    goals for, 81–84
    hiring and, 81
    individuality and, 82, 83
    parents and, 76–77, 78–79,
        84–85
    size and, 76–77
    trial period for, 78–79
    Vermont Design for Education
        and, 82–83
    volunteer aspect of, 79–80

Bankrolled Educational Oppor-
    tunity, 93–99
    costs of, 95, 97
    eligibility requirements for,
        95–96
    payments under, 96
    regulations for, 96–97
    residency and, 95, 96n.
    vouchers and, 97

Basic knowledge, 106
Becket, Massachusetts, 64–65
Berkeley, California, remodeling project, 58
Berkshire School District, Massachusetts, 64–65
Birthday-entrance plan, 23–29
  complaints anticipated for, 28
  costs of, 26–27
  enrollment "bulge" and, 26–27
  grades and, 23, 24
  group processing and, 25–26, 28
  individuality and, 24, 25, 26
  practicality of, 24–25
  statistical projections for, 27
  subversive power of, 25–26
Bond issues, 62
Boston, renovation project in, 58
Boston Globe, 108
Budget
  autonomous-school plan and, 80
  birthday-entrance plan and, 27, 28
  See also Costs
Buildings
  existing, 55–56
  year-round plan and, 34
  zero construction of, *See* Zero-construction building plan

Cautiousness, 107
Certification, teacher, 15
  See also Licenses
Chicago, remodeling project in, 58
Children Teach Children . , 51n., 52
Choice, public schools of, 120–22

Church-related institutions, public dollars and, 98
Class, professional, 11–12
Classes
  size of, maximum, 41
  See also Grades
Community
  control of schools, 14
  teaching resources in, 47
  See also Parents
Compulsory education, 108
  year-round plan and, 30–31, 32–33
Construction
  leasing vs., 59
  zero, *See* Zero-construction building plan
Contracts
  apprenticeship, 47
  autonomous-school plan and, 79
  performance, 14–15
Conversion of existing facilities, 57–65
  See also Zero-construction building plan
Costs
  of autonomous-school plan, 80
  of bankrolled education, 95, 97
  of birthday-entrance plan, 26–27, 28
  of external-diploma plan, 91
  of high-school-renewal plan, 72
  of year-round learning center, 33–34
Cox, Archibald, 119
Credit, academic, apprenticeships and, 47–48
Cremin, Lawrence, 110
Crisis in the Classroom, 118

Decentralization of schools, 14, 77
Decision-making, parental involvement in, 78–79, 85, 123n.
Desegregation, 108
Detroit, decentralization in, 77
Dewey, John, 30
Diplomas
  equivalency, 88–89, 91n–92n.
  external, 16, 86–92
  general, 113
  job qualification for, 90
  military service, 88–89
  multiple system for, 113n.
  one year of college completed and, 90
  performance vs. time-in-school for, 89
  significance of, 87
  standardization of, 86–87, 88, 90
  state education departments and, 88–89
Discrimination, corrective action for, 104–5
Disestablishment of schools, 117
District school board
  autonomous-school plan and, 79, 80, 84
  bankrolled education and, 95n.
  community control and, 14n.
  construction and, 57
  external-diploma plan and, 89, 90
  most-wanted-teacher plan and, 40, 41
  size problems and, 76–77
  year-round learning center and, 31
Diversity in policy, 122
Dominican students, 66, 67

Dropouts
  benefits from, to school district, 93
  bankrolled education for, 93–99
  costliness of, 94–95
  education owed to, 93–94
  equivalency diplomas and, 89
  national commission on, 108
  in New York City, 112
  programs for, 91

Economic stability, educational success and, 104n.
Educational Facilities Laboratories, 57, 61, 62
Employees of public schools, 11
Enrollment size
  birthday-entrance plan and, 26–27
  school-district size and, 76
Entrance, birthday basis of, 23–29
  See also Birthday-entrance plan
Equivalency diplomas, 88–89, 91n.–92n.
Ethnic problems, 66, 67, 104n.
  See also Minorities
Evaluation of teachers, 38, 40
  autonomous-school plan and, 80, 81, 84
External-diploma plan, 16, 86–92
  conditions for, 89–90
  costs of, 91
  existing programs and, 91

Failure, 21–22, 106, 110
Fantini, Mario D., 120–21

Financing education, 122*n*.
for dropouts, 93–99
See also Costs
Fischer, John, 21
Forced schooling, *See* Compulsory education
Ford Foundation, 57
Found space, 57, 62
Furniture and furnishings, 63–64
Future
construction and, 59–60
research and, 105, 106

Gartner, Alan, 51*n*., 52
General diplomas, 113
G.I. Bill, 94, 98
Goals, reform potential of, 81–84
Gold, August, 62
Governing body, autonomous-school plan and, 80
Grades
birthday entrance and, 23, 24
year-round plan and, 35
Graduation, high school, 86
Greer, Colin, 104
Group processing
birthday-entrance plan and, 25–26, 28
year-round plan and, 35
Guards, security, 74–75

Harlem Prep, 58
Harrington, Michael, 108, 111
High school
diplomas, 86–92. *See also* Diplomas.
suburban, 68
See also Secondary schools

High-school-renewal plan, 66–75
advisers for, 69, 72
costs of, 72
ethnic problems and, 66–67
moratorium on conventional work and, 71, 72
planning for, 68–70
principals and, 68, 69, 70
steps for, 68–69
teachers and, 72
Hope for reform, 117–25
Howe, Harold, 109*n*.

Illich, Ivan, 117
Immigrants, 104*n*.
Income, teachers', *See* Salaries, teachers'
Incremental reformers, 106
Individuality
autonomous-school plan and, 82, 83
birthday-entrance plan and, 24, 25, 26
building size and, 56
year-round plan and, 35–36
Information, 106
Integration, racial, 108
See also Minorities
Interest, learning and, 46, 50

"Jews," 104*n*.
Job qualification for diploma, 89, 90

Keppel, Francis, 109*n*.
Kindergarten, birthday-entrance plan and, 27

Kohl, Herb, 120n.
Kohler, Mary, 51n., 52

Lachman, Seymour P., 104n.,
    105, 106
Latin American students, 66, 67
Laymen, 12n.
    See also Parents
Leadership, 103–14
    parents and, 122, 123–25
    survivalist, 110
Learning
    center, year-round, 30–36
    children, from other children,
        52
    interest and, 46, 50
Leasing, construction vs., 59
Legislation
    for apprenticed-learner plan,
        50
    teachers' opposition to, 119–20
Licenses
    nonschool teachers and, 48–49
    review for, 15, 37n.
Lock-step schooling, 23
    year-round plan and, 35

Make your own plan, 100
Marland, Sidney P., Jr., 94n.
Maximum class size, most-
    wanted-teacher plan and, 41
Merit pay, 38–39
Military service, diplomas and,
    88–89
Minorities, 104–5
    autonomous-school plan and,
        79n.
    high-school renewal and, 66–
        67

Minorities (cont.)
    integration and, 108
Moderation in school manage-
    ment, 103–5, 106
Most-wanted-teacher plan, 37–45
    accountability and, 45
    assistants under, 41, 42
    computations under, 41
    dismissals under, 42
    evaluation and, 38, 40
    maximum class size and, 41
    parents and, 39, 40–41
    problem areas in, 42
    resistance to, anticipated, 44
    salaries and, 37–45
    secondary schools and, 40n.

National Commission on the Re-
    form of Secondary Educa-
    tion, 108
New York City, 112–14
    accountability committee in,
        16n.
    citizens' organization in, 112
    conversion of buildings in, 58–
        59, 62–64
    decentralization in, 14, 77
    dropouts in, 112
    equivalency diplomas in, 91n.–
        92n.
    failure of system in, 112–14
    moderation in, 103, 106n.
    promotion in, 109
    scope of system in, 112

On-the-job qualification for
    diploma, 89, 90
Options, 108
"Other America," 108, 111

Otis, Massachusetts, 65
Out-of-school students, 46–50

Parents, 16
autonomous-school plan and,
76–77, 78–79, 84–85
community control and, 14
decision-making and, 78–79,
85, 123n.
hope for reform and, 122,
123–25
most-wanted-teacher plan and,
39, 40–41
peer tutoring and, 54
planning and, 68–69, 71
rights of, 44
size of school districts and, 76–
77
year-round schools and, 32, 34
Peer tutoring, 51–54
Performance
contracting, 14–15
salaries and, 37–45
vs. time-in-school for diploma,
89, 90
Philadelphia, remodeling project
in, 58
Planning, 106
involvement in, 68–71
Plans, reform, See Reform plans
Police, 74–75
Poverty, 111–12
failure and, 104
peer tutoring and, 54
Principals, 68, 69, 70
See also Administrators
Probationary teachers, 15
Professionals, school, 11–17
certification and, 15. See also
Licenses

Professionals, school (cont.)
class interests of, 11–12
community control and, 14
control by, 12
parents' relationships with, 14
performance contracting and,
14–15
problem-solving by, 12–13
resistance of, to reform, 13–17,
119
seniority rights and, 15–16
Promotions, New York procedure
for, 109
Public schools of choice, 120–22
Purpose of public schools, 11, 17

Racial integration, 108
See also Minorities
Radical reform, 99, 105, 106
Reading problems
promotion and, 109, 110
youth tutoring and, 52
Recession, seniority rights and,
15
Reform
administrators and, 109–10
Allen's proposals for, 98–99
cautiousness and, 107
common sense and, 99
discrimination and, 104–5
Fantini view of, 120–21
goals and, 81–84
hope for, 117–25
Illich vision of, 117
incremental, 106
leadership for, 103-14
moderation and, 103-5, 106
parents and, 122, 123–25
public schools of choice and,
120–22

Reform (*cont.*)
  radical, 99, 105, 106
  resistance to, 13–17, 119
  Silberman view of, 117–20
Reform plans
  apprenticed-learner, 46–50
  autonomous-school, 76–85
  bankrolled-education, 93–99
  birthday-entrance, 23–29
  external-diploma, 86–92
  high-school-renewal, 66–75
  make your own, 100
  most-wanted-teacher, 37–45
  submission of, 100
  universal-tutor, 51–54
  year-round-learning-center, 30–36
  zero-construction building, 55–65
Relicensing, 15, 37*n.*
Research, educational, 105, 106, 107
Residency requirement, bankrolled education and, 95, 96*n.*
Resistance to reform, 13–17, 119
Retention rights of teachers, 15
Review of teachers, 15, 37*n.*
  See also Evaluation of teachers
Revisionists, 104
Riessman, Frank, 51*n.*, 52
Rights
  public schools of choice and, 121
  seniority, 15–16
  of students, 44

Salaries, teachers'
  merit pay and, 38–39
  performance and, 37–45

Scandinavian-Americans, 104*n.*–105*n.*
School board, *See* District school board
School systems, concept of two, 110–15
Schrag, Peter, 106
Science, 106
Scribner, Harvey
  accountability committee and, 16*n.*
  address (mailing) of, 100
  apprenticed-learner plan and, 50*n.*
  birthday-entrance plan (Teaneck) and, 25*n.*
  parental involvement and, 78*n.*
Secondary schools
  national commission on, 108
  tutors from, 53
  See also High school; High-school-renewal plan
Security guards, 74–75
Segregation, racial, 108
  See also Minorities
Seniority rights of teachers, 15–16
Shanker, Albert, 14, 106*n.*
Silberman, Charles E., 117–20
Size, problems of, 76–77
Springfield *Union*, 64
Standards
  diplomas and, 86–87, 88, 90
  reading problems and, 109
State education departments
  bankrolled education and, 95, 96, 97
  equivalency diplomas and, 88–89
Stevens, Leonard, 50*n.*

Students
  apprenticeships for, 46–50
  assignment of, 43
  Dominican, 66, 67
  failure of, 14–15, 21–22
  interest of, 46
  needs of, purpose of schools
    and, 11, 17
  out-of-school, 46–50
  performance contracting and,
    14–15
  planning and, 68–69, 70, 71
  rights of, 44
  as tutors, 51–54
  volunteer, 33
Suburban high schools, 68
Summer-closing tradition, 34
Survivalist leadership, 110

Taxes, bankrolled education and,
    97
Teachers
  autonomous-school plan and,
    83
  dismissals of, 42
  evaluation of, 38, 40, 80, 81,
    84
  high-school-renewal plan and,
    72
  licenses of, 15, 37n., 48–49
  most-wanted, 37–45
  nonschool, 46–50
  organizational power of, 119
  probationary, 15
  resistance of, to reform, 13–17,
    119
  retention rights of, 15
  review of, 15, 37n.
  salary of, 37–45
  seniority rights of, 15–16

Teachers (cont.)
  unlicensed, 48–49
  as victims, 118–19
  year-round plan and, 33, 34–35
Teaneck, New Jersey, 25n.
Tutors, students as, 51–54
Two school systems, concept of,
    110–15

United Federation of Teachers
    (New York), 14n., 119
Universal-tutor plan, 51–54
Universities
  birthday-entrance plan and, 27
  equivalency diplomas and, 89,
    90
  licensing and, 37n.
  student-tutors from, 53
  year-round plan and, 35
Urban school failures, 104–5

Vacations, year-round plan and,
    34
Vermont Design for Education,
    82–83
Veterans
  G.I. Bill and, 94, 98
  programs for, 91
Violence in schools, 66–67
Voluntary participation
  autonomous-school plan and,
    79–80
  year-round plan and, 31, 33
Vouchers, 97, 120

Words, reality of, 105
Work performance, diploma and,
    89, 90

Year-round-learning-center plan,
30–36
advance notice and, 32
advantages of, 34
building use and, 34
compulsory-attendance law
and, 30–31, 32–33
costs of, 33–34
group processing and, 35
individuality and, 35–36
limitation of attendance in, 34,
35
personnel requirements of, 33,
34–35
rationale for, 32–33
subversive potential of, 35
vacations and, 34
voluntary nature of, 31, 33

Zero-construction building plan,
55–65
bond issues and, 62
check list for, 60–61
Educational Facilities Laboratories and, 57, 61, 62
existing structures and, 55–59,
61
found space and, 57, 62
furniture and furnishings and,
63–64
future educational commit-
ments and, 59–60
individuality and, 56
leasing space and, 58–59
priorities and, educational, 60
reorganization and, 61, 62–
63

ABOUT THE AUTHORS

HARVEY B. SCRIBNER has taught in a one-room schoolhouse in Maine and run the largest public-school system in the United States. He has been a classroom teacher, elementary-school principal, high-school principal, superintendent of schools, state commissioner of education (Vermont), university teacher, and college trustee. He was the first Chancellor of the New York City public schools, from 1970 to 1973. Born in Albion, Maine, he earned his doctorate at Boston University at the age of forty-five. Dr. Scribner currently teaches at the University of Massachusetts and is a Senior Lecturer for Nova University's doctoral program for educational leaders. He and his wife, Alta, live in Amherst, Massachusetts.

LEONARD B. STEVENS has been writing about, working in or studying schools and school policy issues for more than ten years. From 1970 to 1973 he was Special Assistant to the Chancellor of the New York City public schools, Harvey Scribner. He has received several awards from the Education Writers Association. Mr. Stevens is currently working on a doctoral degree at the University of Massachusetts. He and his wife, Bette, have three children, Lisa, Christopher and Andrew.

ONE OF OUR MOST experienced and innovative public educators, the first Chancellor of the New York City Public Schools, here describes some practical, playful, imaginative and cost-free plans that parents can campaign for *right away*, and that could turn public education around *starting right now*.

To begin with, Scribner and Stevens ask a lot of questions about our schools that are so simple and obvious that most of us haven't thought of asking them. When we do, it becomes clear that schools are run by rules that have nothing to do with teaching people, that waste money and talent, and that center around the needs of the staff rather than of the students.

Why do all kids have to start school for the first time on the same day? Why do they all have to go to the same classrooms for the same 180 days a year? Why can't the students and their parents decide which teachers and which schools are successful? Why do children have to sit in classrooms when sometimes the very people who know how to do what the youngsters want to learn are out on the job doing it and could teach them there and then? Why can't the energies of young people be tapped to teach each other? Why are we wasting money on buildings we don't need when we have better uses for the money? Why should diplomas and other credentials be awarded only for what is learned inside a classroom and only before the age of 18; why shouldn't we be able to collect our education rights any time we want to?

If we get rid of some of our inherited baggage and outworn habits by asking these

(continued on back flap)